THE DOUBLE AXE
AND OTHER POEMS

THE DOUBLE AXE

AND OTHER POEMS
INCLUDING ELEVEN
SUPPRESSED POEMS

BY

ROBINSON JEFFERS

With a Foreword by William Everson
and an Afterword by Bill Hotchkiss

LIVERIGHT
New York   London

Published simultaneously in Canada by Penguin Books
Canada Ltd, 2801 John Street, Markham, Ontario
L3R 1B4
Printed in the United States of America.

From *Selected Poems* by Robinson Jeffers. Copyright
© 1965 by Donnan and Garth Jeffers. Reprinted by
permission of Random House, Inc.: "Their Beauty Has
More Meaning," "Cassandra," "Original Sin," "The
Inquisitors," "Advice to Pilgrims," "Calm and Full the
Ocean," "The Eye," "Teheran," " So Many Blood-
Lakes," "Diagram," and "We Are Those People."

Library of Congress Cataloging in Publication Data
Jeffers, Robinson, 1887–1962.
    The double axe, and other poems, including eleven
suppressed poems.
    I. Title.
PC3519.E27D6 1977 811'.5'2   76–55796

ISBN 0-87140-114-2

Liveright Publishing Corporation,
500 Fifth Avenue, New York, N.Y. 10110
W. W. Norton & Company Ltd.,
37 Great Russell Street, London WC1B 3NU

3 4 5 6 7 8 9 0

CONTENTS

CONTENTS

FOREWORD

I

When Robinson Jeffers first broke upon the literary
scene, humanist critics indicted his "amoral" philosophy.
With the whole body of his work before us, however, it is
apparent that on the contrary his moral stance was posi-
tively forbidding, gaining its power from an almost pri-
mordial sense of Original Sin. Denied by Darwin the
theological sanction of his Calvinist forebears, he yet re-
tained its thrust by positing an evolutionary aberration
in the history of the species, a genetic flaw, a biological
wrong turn taken. The breed has something botched about
it, and whoever would follow its tendencies walks with
devils. No other animal, he averred, is so instinctually
perverse, so corrupted by self-love.

And like an intrepid desert prophet he set about the
correction, writing poems which were massive acts of con-
frontation, exhortation, and persuasion. He confronted
human pride with the facts of human abjectness, he ex-
horted human complacency with acts of religious arousal,
and he persuaded of human folly by appeal to transhu-
man relevance. Thus he sought to wrench man's attention
from his own self-deceptions, and fasten his soul upon
the naked divinity manifest in the cosmos. This is a fa-
miliar enough religious tactic, but Jeffers' employment
of it is extraordinary. Nineteenth-century science had
presented Nietzsche with a universe in which there was no
place left for God. Twentieth-century science presented
Jeffers with a universe in which there is no place left for
man.[1]

1. It was the discovery in 1924 that the spiral nebulae, for-
merly thought to be part of the Milky Way, are in fact distinct
galaxies, infinitely expanding man's conception of the cosmos,
that clinched Jeffers' sense of human insignificance.

For unquestionably it was science that provided him with the objectivity, and hence the authority, to effect the religious mission he claimed for his own—particularly the sciences of astronomy and physics. Between those two millstones, the galaxy and the molecule, he pulverized human complacency to reveal man's insignificance to man. Whereas religious humanists like T. S. Eliot resisted the tendency of science to displace humanity from the center of things, Jeffers welcomed it and, moreover, celebrated it. He turned the employ of science back from the proliferation of creature comforts to religious contemplation; and what it contemplated was virtually ungraspable, a vision "measureless to man."

The principal dispositive factor which Jeffers acquired from science was detachment, deepening to aloofness and, at times, remoteness. This made for a profound antipathy to the affairs of man. From such disinvolvement only two areas emerge in which he succumbed to the participation he disdained: the Eros-Thanatos equation presented by fundamental biology. Because sex is personal and private, he was able to keep it in focus, though it constantly threatened to overwhelm his objectivity: in all his work it has a luridity and glare that emphasize its dangerous aspects. So too with death, personal death. Neither rejecting it philosophically nor seeking it through suicide, he kept it in stern focus. But collective death, vast impersonal death in the form of universal war—this was too much for him. The first and second world wars were the two crisis periods of his life, wherein he lost detachment and plunged into intense psychological involvement. In World War I his powers were not yet mature, and the record is unclear. But in World War II he stood upon the stage of contemporary literature and believed he had to speak out.[2]

2. James Shebl, in *In This Wild Water: The Suppressed Poems of Robinson Jeffers* (Pasadena, 1976), argues that

For in the throes of the latter he could not forget the treasons of the former. At high-level conferences like Teheran and Yalta he could not forget high-level betrayals like Versailles. Disdaining and disavowing politics, he yet became, confronted with these episodes, a political poet. This began as far back as the early thirties with the first signs of the drift toward war in Europe. In the poem "Rearmament," published in 1935 but written apparently in 1934 when Stalin announced Russian rearmament, he declared:

> These grand and fatal movements toward death:
>   the grandeur of the mass
> Makes pity a fool, the tearing pity
> For the atoms of the mass, the persons, the
>   victims, make it seem monstrous
> To admire the tragic beauty they build.[3]

Here the stance is aloof but already the involvement is unmistakable. Thirteen years later, in the present book, *The Double Axe*, he would give us that involvement projected to its apotheosis, a paroxysm of anguished revulsion.

As a genre political poetry is both didactic and rhetorical. To be effective it must be intensely involved and ideologically committed, though such commitment must be moderated by intellectual discrimination, moral courage, and, sometimes, irony. Within these bounds it is best when it is extreme: intemperate, explosive, and scornful. In-

---

Jeffers' resort to current political incidents was not so much an abandonment of detachment as a legitimate device for grounding his Inhumanist philosophy in reality. Without denying this, I base my own point of view rather on a manifest shift in Jeffers' mood. With the approach of war in the thirties he began to speak not in terms of what *is* but in terms of what *ought to be*.

3. "Rearmament," *The Selected Poetry of Robinson Jeffers* (New York, 1938), p. 565.

deed, unless it invokes the leap for the jugular, we are not apt to pay much attention to it. Only when it shocks with relevance can it change the course of human inertia. Being poetry, it must be concentrated and blistering rather than rational and discursive, or we will cling to prose and remain in dispassionate analysis. As an axiom it can be said that the rougher political poetry is, the better we will like it, or, if it opposes our own predilections, the more deeply will we fear it. Political poetry speaks to the mind, certainly, but at best it speaks *through* the mind to the passions. In spite of ourselves, hearing it, we are moved.

In *The Double Axe*, Jeffers proves himself to be a political poet par excellence, an adept at the rougher aspects of political infighting. The howls of rage from his opponents testify to it. No other contemporary verse comes to mind that is quite so brusque, savage, and intransigent. What anti-war poetry of the sixties, for instance, equals "Eagle Valor, Chicken Mind" for incisiveness? The rhetorical skills he had developed denigrating the race were focused now on deploring the course of political issue, and if he could cow the species before the vision of God, he could certainly shatter the pretensions of crusading politicos before the awesome eventualities of their options. When he finished his book and signed his name to it, he put his signature on a death warrant.

But though history may yet vindicate him, in terms of his poetic career his descent into the political arena was an unmitigated disaster. For one thing, political poetry itself was then out of fashion. In the thirties the Depression had produced a bond between political radicals and creative writers founded, as in the sixties, upon an anti-war rhetoric. This was cynically fostered by the Communist party up through the Stalin-Hitler nonaggression pact of 1939. With the collapse of that détente in 1941, followed by Pearl Harbor, the demoralized Left was assimilated into the war effort, the Communists jubilant, the dissidents succumbing to the doctrinaire tactic of "boring from within," a formula successful enough when used by the Bolsheviks in the defeated czarist armies of World War I, but utterly ineffectual amongst the confident GIs of World War II. On the home front the unenlisted dissident literati were reduced to grinding out government propaganda or retiring into hermeticism and the cultivation of aesthetic form. By the battle of Midway, the turning point of the war, *Literature and Revolution* was out and *Seven Types of Ambiguity* was in.[4]

Moreover, in 1948 the nation at large was enjoying an interval of rare self-esteem. Victory had proved American justice and she stood before the world as the savior of mankind. All the free nations looked to her for security and protection, and she felt worthy of it. She saw the ordeal of her triumph as heroic and self-sacrificial, and after very real privations she was enjoying the reward of an accelerating prosperity.

Into this bland, complacent atmosphere Jeffers' book dropped like a bomb (a stink bomb, many thought). Certainly the reaction was violent enough. How dare this intransigent curmudgeon vilify the great ordeal of victory by such discredited isolationist ranting? His own publisher held his nose and quarantined the book with a pious disclaimer. Hustled out of decent society with antiseptics and rubber gloves, *The Double Axe* was universally consigned to oblivion, effectively ending Jeffers' role as a creditable poetic voice during his lifetime.[5]

Yet only the year before, Jeffers had ridden to the high

4. "Five years or so ago, hot young Trotskyite lady organizers had a habit of, without warning, giving up the Revolution for Ransom's *Kenyon Review,* and nobody thought the worse of them for it." Kenneth Rexroth, "Letter from America," *Now,* no. 7 (London, Autumn, 1946), p. 65.

5. Shebl (op. cit.) explores Jeffers' difficulties with his publisher in depth.

point of his career with the stage success of his Greek adaptation, *Medea*. Night after night it had played to full houses, continuing month in and month out, lauded by the country's most respected drama critics, publicized in newspapers and magazines all over the country. It was generally acknowledged to be the postwar high point of legitimate theatre in this country.

Jeffers onstage was something new, but the literary critics, long familiar with his voice, had not been so hospitable to the play's appearance in book form. Now, with the publication of *The Double Axe*, it was as if the *Medea* success had never happened. The play had no political overtones, but this new book was loaded, and the watchdogs bristled. "A necrophilic nightmare!" cried *Time* magazine, and a host of compeers bayed in response. "His gruesome puppets," declared *The New Yorker*, "have only melodramtic impact and no appeal." The *Virginia Kirkus Book Service* condemned it as "the latest Robinson Jeffers cocktail—one part Sophocles, one part Lone Ranger, a dash of William Faulkner, and plenty of bitters . . . puerile and violent rodomontade." "His violent political isolation," intoned the Cleveland *Press*, "is divorced from what people think. . . . Jeffers is breathing, but he is asleep." The St. Louis *Dispatch* protested that "Jeffers is hopelessly isolated from life and unbalanced in his thinking . . . only the most devout followers of the right-wing nationalists, the lunatic fringe, and the most ardent Roosevelt haters, could, after reading *The Double Axe*, welcome the return of Robinson Jeffers." The Milwaukee *Journal* said, "In this truculent book, Robinson Jeffers . . . makes it clear that he feels the human race should be abolished." And the San Francisco *Chronicle* opined that "we have one of the most powerful word-craftsmen of our time dipping his pen in international pus in an effort to write what, philosophically, amounts to a cosmic sequel to *Black Beauty*."

These cries of outrage and indignation echoed across the land. The *New York Times Book Review* praised a few passages in the shorter poems, "but they are scarcely enough to redeem the apoplectic shouting of the rest." "The attitude is childish and childishly easy," admonished the *New Republic*, "a sorry exhibition for a responsible poet to have made." The St. Paul *Dispatch* said that "whatever Jeffers' gifts may have once been, the ability to write verse has deserted him. . . . No lines quite so blunt, heavy-footed, and prosy ever masqueraded as poetry quite so unpersuasively." *Voices*, the poetry magazine, condemned the unrelieved violence and horror of the title poem. The short poems are "repetitious and flat," Jeffers has lost his "old sweep and power," and "the path he has chosen seems to be leading at present through very barren territory." The *Nation* called it typical Jeffers, a long narrative poem with horrible characters, and deeds of lurid violence on practically every page. The *Library Journal* said "his violent, hateful book is a gospel of isolationism carried beyond geography, faith or hope." The Los Angeles *Times* called it "the most violent antiwar poetry ever published in this country. . . . The narrative poem is weak in plot and characters and almost barren of the poetry of place which ennobles Jeffers' best work." And in conclusion the *Saturday Review of Literature*, while recalling his past esteem, found it sad that "he feels compelled to add more than his quota of hatred and violence to the hatred and violence abroad in the world, while he sits in that properly inhuman stone tower of his waiting exultantly for the Bomb."[6]

Jeffers predicted this rejection for more than twenty years, but it is interesting that what his religious invective could not effect his political invective accomplished

6. The foregoing synopsis of reviews is taken from Alex A. Vardamis, *The Critical Reputation of Robinson Jeffers* (Hamden, Conn., 1972), pp. 108–114.

overnight. A prophet may announce the end of the world from the housetops and the authorities will yawn. But let him announce the end of the status quo and his days are numbered.

Of the political content which produced this reaction little need be said. It pleads from the text, requiring no elucidation, only summarization. Jeffers believed American participation in World War II was a tragic mistake, wasting American lives and resources to fish in what he considered the witches' brew of Europe—a venerable American sentiment, to be sure, but expressed with such bluntness, and now timed so awkwardly, as to incense rather than convince. This was Jeffers' forte as a religious poet; it was his nemesis as a political one. Still, he made his points. The triumphant liberal slogans of those years he ruthlessly excoriated. All the presuppositions of post-war One World enthusiasm he punctured with powerful invective.

These issues are still with us today, and the republication of *The Double Axe* will doubtless provoke a corresponding reaction, though hardly to the same degree. Nevertheless, it is in his dual role as prophet no less than poet that Jeffers continues to interest. The first interest is environmental. The ecological crisis has driven home with great force the pertinence of Jeffers' insistence that man divorced from nature is a monstrosity. By wrenching attention from man to cosmos he has served as a powerful counterbalance to perennial human egocentricity, and his witness in this regard is only beginning. No matter what civilizations survive this one, the pertinence of his vision will go on, because it is not possible to state the case more emphatically.

The second interest is political. In the wake of our disillusionment with Vietnam it is sobering to read how accurately Jeffers foresaw the predicament America is now facing in the world, despite the charge of the St. Louis

Dispatch, previously noted, that his affinity was with "the right-wing nationalists, the lunatic fringe, and the most ardent Roosevelt haters." This strain is there, certainly, but the deeper message lives on, as America seeks to retrench itself along lines that are politically and militarily tenable, confronting a circle of hostile nations that once were friends.

> Two bloody summers from now (I suppose) we
> shall have to take up the corrupting burden
> and curse of victory.
> We shall have to hold half the earth, we shall
> be sick with self-disgust,
> And hated by friend and foe, and hold half the
> earth—or let it go and go down with it.[7]

America does not yet accept Jeffers' thesis that its present difficulties stem from a tragic misadventure, the entering of World War II, following the incipient tragic error of involvement in World War I. But at least his utterances now fall on more receptive ears than the deaf ones which spurned his words when he was still alive to speak.[8]

Thus, tentatively, but with deepening interest, the world is beginning to reapproach Robinson Jeffers, having first found him too hot and then too cold. For it is his extremes that are attractive. As John Burroughs said of Thoreau, "He improves with age—in fact requires age to take off a little of his asperity, and fully ripen him. The world likes a good hater and refuser almost as well as it likes a good lover and acceptor—only it likes him farther off."[9]

7. "Historical Choice," *The Double Axe,* p. 129.

8. The recent publication of certain of these poems in *Harper's* (February, 1976, pp. 45–46) under the heading "Making the Nightmare Make Sense," by Robert Ian Scott, indicates that perhaps Jeffers' point, so long deferred, may at last find a hearing.

9. Quoted by Walt Whitman in *Specimen Days* (Boston, 1971), p. 113.

II

The Double Axe is divided into three parts. The title
poem itself is made up of two related but markedly dis-
tinct narratives, followed by a section of shorter poems.
The first of the narratives and the short poems go to-
gether; written during the war or just after it, they both
share the same past. "The Love and the Hate" is a blend
of two familiar Jeffers motifs: the return of the dead to
accost the living with beyond-the-grave prescience, and
the return of the Oedipal son out of hatred of his father
and desire for his mother: what Radcliffe Squires has
dubbed "the destroying prodigal" archetype. By blend-
ing these two strains together, Jeffers increases impression
to the breaking point, passing beyond anything he had
previously dared in disgust and revulsion. It takes a
strong stomach to get through it. Among many appalling
incidents, its most memorable passage is the address of
the prodigal as he accosts his father and sums up with
great vehemence the case of disenchanted youth against
the merely politically adventitious aspects of the war.
Perhaps nothing in modern letters speaks so bluntly of
the negative side of the American penchant for project-
ing its ideals on the world as this boy's devastating pre-
diction. It constitutes the central point, the focus around
which the entire book revolves.

The second narrative, however, "The Inhumanist,"
looks to the future, and in terms of Jeffers' over-all de-
velopment it is unprecedented, unique in that its spirit is
comic rather than tragic. In fact, it is hardly a narrative
at all, more of a series of meditations on incidents that re-
flect the ordeal of worldly involvement, events seeking
out a recluse in spite of his withdrawal. If "The Love and
the Hate" is the darkest narrative Jeffers ever penned,
then "The Inhumanist" is, by far, the lightest. How ex-
plain this? What produced such a striking dichotomy

between Jeffers' political disgust and this transpolitical benignity which is so engaging?

I believe the answer to the second part of the question is found in the first, namely, that involvement itself produced its opposite. "The Love and the Hate" was written in wartime in 1944; "The Inhumanist" was written in the aftermath, the year of peace 1947, and it more or less acknowledges that his involvement in political dispute had violated his primary principle of aloofness. Was he motivated, therefore, to create a figure which, since aloofness had been jeopardized, meets secular involvement in consonance with his own long-standing principles? If so, in doing this he has created, despite himself, something suspiciously like a savior figure—not in the traditional religious sense of a Buddha or a Jesus, of course, but along the Nietzschean lines of a Zarathustra—a savior figure, that is, who constitutes some kind of model for human conduct, an intellectual and moral attitude appropriate to mankind in the dilemma of existence which now confronts it.

This is significant because Jeffers spent a good part of his creative energy inveighing against saviors, whom he realized to be the spearhead of humanist-oriented religious consciousness. Thus the poem has profound implications which cast their light far down Jeffers' earlier achievement, clear back to *The Women at Point Sur*, where he first thrust the savior ideal against the naked stars and watched it warp before his eyes. There, since the poem, his own creation, arranged the determining content, he could see to it that the ideal broke utterly under the torsion of objective reality, and so it happened. Thus emboldened, he next turned his attention to the central religious figure in Western consciousness, the person of Christ, and in *Dear Judas* reduced it to an ordeal of self-delusion, efficacious insofar as Jesus served powers greater than He knew, but pathetic insofar as He misconceived (as Jeffers thought) His own role in history. With such a victory under his belt, Jeffers could well afford to assume that the savior archetype had been adequately explained and effectively controverted.

However, in the light of his own involvement, that would no longer do. In *The Double Axe* he had to create a figure that would encompass involvement, conceding responsibility to mankind while at the same time defining its limits, and so he created the nameless old man, the only viable savior figure in his writing. The surfacing of the redeemer archetype here is revealing, given Jeffers' efforts to deny it. It derives from his own descent into the political arena. Perhaps he is conceived so as to save Jeffers from himself, from his own political involvement in "The Love and the Hate." But at the very least it indicates the survivability, not to say the indestructibility, of the savior archetype in human consciousness, an archetype which, as we saw, Jeffers had taken great pains to disavow—and continues to disavow in the words of his hero even as he creates him. But the salvific instance has been achieved, this is what is important. For one thing, it enables Jeffers to lighten his tone, and even flicker his narrative with traces of humor.

What this indicates regarding his earlier attempts is still moot: the full work of exegesis exploring the range of implication across the body of his writing must await the patience of future scholars. For the contemporary reader, however, it is enough to say that if the old man is not the most awesome of Jeffers' protagonists, he is certainly the most genial and hospitable. In the long roster of forbidding Jeffersian characters he is a delight.

*

In these two narratives, then, the reader will find the extremes of one of the most resistant and sheerly faceted contemporary literary figures. If "The Love and the Hate" may qualify as his most gruesome work, then "The

Inhumanist" is his most serene. In the former the mask slips, and a bitter political animus glints through. But in "The Inhumanist" the reader will see the genial side of the man as he never elsewhere permitted it to emerge, a confident and hopeful celebration of what humankind can be capable of if it will only stop the fever of self-involvement, and contemplate the living God.

WILLIAM EVERSON

ACKNOWLEDGMENTS

The editors gratefully acknowledge the cooperation of Random House; Donnan Jeffers; David Farmer; Humanities Research Center, University of Texas, Austin; James M. Shebl; Robert Ian Scott; and *Harper's* Magazine.

PREFACE

The first part of *The Double Axe* was written during the war and finished a year before the war ended, and it bears the scars; but the poem is not primarily concerned with that grim folly. Its burden, as of some previous work of mine, is to present a certain philosophical attitude, which might be called Inhumanism, a shifting of emphasis and significance from man to not-man; the rejection of human solipsism and recognition of the transhuman magnificence. It seems time that our race began to think as an adult does, rather than like an egocentric baby or insane person. This manner of thought and feeling is neither misanthropic nor pessimist, though two or three people have said so and may again. It involves no falsehoods, and is a means of maintaining sanity in slippery times; it has objective truth and human value. It offers a reasonable detachment as rule of conduct, instead of love, hate and envy. It neutralizes fanaticism and wild hopes; but it provides magnificence for the religious instinct, and satisfies our need to admire greatness and rejoice in beauty.

The shorter poems that tail the book are expressions, in their different ways, of the same attitude. A few of them have been printed previously; three in *Poetry Magazine*, one in the *University of Kansas City Review*, two in *The Saturday Review of Literature;* several in some recent anthologies.

As to the Publishers' Note that introduces this volume, let me say that it is here with my cheerful consent, and represents a quite normal difference of opinion. But I believe that history (though not popular history) will eventually take sides with me in these matters. Surely it is clear even now that the whole world would be better off if America had refrained from intervention in the European war of 1914; I think it will become equally clear that our intervention in the Second World War has been—even terribly—worse in effect. And this intervention was not forced but intentional; we were making war, in fact though not in name, long before Pearl Harbor. But it is futile at present to argue these matters. And they are not particularly important, so far as this book is concerned; they are only the background, or moral climate, of its thought and action.

R. J.

PUBLISHERS' NOTE

THE DOUBLE AXE AND OTHER POEMS is the fourteenth book of verse by Robinson Jeffers published under the Random House imprint.* During an association of fifteen years, marked by mutual confidence and accord, the issuance of each new volume has added strength to the close relationship of author and publisher. In all fairness to that constantly interdependent relationship and in complete candor, Random House feels compelled to go on record with its disagreement over some of the political views pronounced by the poet in this volume. Acutely aware of the writer's freedom to express his convictions boldly and forthrightly and of the publisher's function to obtain for him the widest possible hearing, whether there is agreement in principle and detail or not, it is of the utmost importance that difference of views should be wide open on both sides. Time alone is the court of last resort in the case of ideas on trial.

* Actually the first of these (*Tamar and Other Poems*) was published by Peter G. Boyle at the poet's expense. The next six were published under the Boni & Liveright, Horace Liveright, or Liveright imprints and transferred to Random House in 1933 along with *Give Your Heart to the Hawks,* then in galley proof. [Editors' note]

THE DOUBLE AXE

I

THE LOVE AND THE HATE

A FIRE a few years before had skinned the
    hills' faces,
    And Nature played one of her beautiful
tricks;
She planted them solidly with purple lupin, sheets of pure
  blossom
From peak to base, so that they stood like archangels
Above the shadow in the canyon, their purple shoulders
In the blue sky.
      Summer came on, earth dried, grass
    whitened,
The lupin hills that had darkened like withdrawing gods
    in the evenings in April
Were now turned brown; they had their beauty; they
    were great brown-furred animals walking across
The pale blue sky. Reine walked below them and thought
It was interesting the seed of two men could mingle
So kindly in her, without shame or disturbance; and it
    was interesting
That she was falling in love with her young lover, not at
    first but now, young again, young and avid
As a young bride.

                    She had been with him,
And when they parted he walked up the ridge beside her
To the lip of the canyon, leading his horse,
And there turned back. She came down alone against the
          sun-glare
And its track on the ocean, and did not see
Until she was in the dooryard, and then half-dazzled, a
          man, a soldier,
Standing beside the stilted water-tank, the Spanish girl
Peeking at him from the doorway. Reine looked again
And screamed, "Hoult. O my God, Hoult!" and ran to
          him
And embraced him. He was cold and stiff in response;
          he had always been shy
Of her flighty tenderness—and held his face
Higher than her head. She babbled, "Darling, why didn't
          you
Let us know you were coming? Where have you been?
How did you get . . . like this . . ." For his tight-
          buttoned
Tunic was wet and stained, filthy to smell,
And he'd not said a word yet. "Did you . . . are you
          hurt? Oh, Hoult,
What have they done to you?" He still not answering,
          she pressed
Her cheek on the stained cloth over his heart:
"Oh! I'm so happy!" "Yeh," he said, "I came home.
All hell couldn't've stopped me. The will does it. What
          were you
Doing on the hill?" "Darling," she said, "can you stay
          long?

                          4

Have you been sick? You look . . . dreadful." He said,
    "Like something
Dug up? I know." "Oh," she said, "you look as if you'd
    been sick.
Did you catch that malaria? Let's go in-doors.
I love you dear." "What were you doing on the hill,
    Mother?"
"What?" she said. "You mean just now? I was taking a
    walk.
Time hangs heavy and lonesome when there is nobody:
But now it won't. How long can you stay?" He said,
"As long as I damn please. So there was nobody?" She
    remembered the light-glare,
To her eyes but not his adverse, but at that distance . . .
And David had surely not come to the open ridge-top:
"What is the matter, dear? Of course there was nobody.
Do you mean you're out of the Army, they've let you go?
You're free, you're free?" His brown eyes and her blue
    ones
Fed on each other in the light air, and she saw the sick
Greenish-dark skin hang on the bones of his face. "Yeh,"
    he said,
"Out." He turned from her and spat; the spittle
Looked lead-color and fell like a lump
On the scuffed earth. "Liar," he said. She mourned, "Oh,
    Hoult!
What has happened to you?" "If you hadn't lied to me
    I would've told you.
Where's the old man?" "I," she said, ". . . Monterey.
American Legion supper. I remember now
I did see someone; I didn't remember.
A friend of yours: Dave Larson: passed me on the trail.

5

He was probably hunting wild pigs."

                                    The black-haired girl
Jesusa, whom they called Hazel, approximating
The sound of the Spanish name—she approached and said
Supper was on the table; and at the same moment
The nutcracker-faced old cowhand Moro Soto
Trotted around a corner of the house, the older of the
        ranch-dogs
Weaving behind his legs, uttering a choked
Continuous howl. Soto said, "My God, you back,"
Offering his hand to shake, "My God, you back again!
You kill some Japs. Ah? Ah?" "No, I got killed,"
He answered, gripping his mother's wrist
Instead of the old man's hand, and he led her captive
Toward the foot of the house-yard, where a dry-stone
        fence
Edges the fall of the gorge. She said, "You hurt me.
What is it with poor old Sport? Speak to him, Hoult.
Doesn't he know you?" "He snarled at me and I booted
        him.
To hell with him. And you. It was Larson, was it,
Tipped you on your back?" "Oh! You're insane," she said,
Wrenching her wrist in his hand in vain. He said, "Okay.
I'm not your keeper. Next time comb the dry fern-bed
Out of your pretty hair." She breathed and said slowly,
        "Some awful thing
Has happened to you. Let me go, Hoult." He said, "You
        guessed it.
There are millions and millions, but as far as I know I am
        the only one
That has come back. It's unbelievable: how can they lie
        so still

After being gypped and killed? Gypped by their govern-
ments
And their fathers and their women: gypped out of life,
fooled and despised and lied to, and stuck
Under the mangrove roots and the black mud, under the
coral sand and the Russian snow,
And the cabbages in Europe. They're too submissive, they
ought to damn patience and rise. Think of the
Stinking armies of semi-skeletons marching on Washing-
ton: here comes your wah," he said, imitating
The President's manner of speech, "here is your wah, you
made it,
How do you like it? While the German boys
Unfox the rock-holes of Berchtesgaden, and all the little
killed Nips nip their Emperor to death—ha? That
would be fine,
That would be justice. But," he said somberly, "justice
Begins at home. So they still have those Legion suppers,
The poor old war-hounds? Ah? The last Saturday
In every month: what a life: I guess we don't lose much
By dying young. It is the lies, it is the lies, it is the dirty
lies,
War-peddlers' lies and the people's imbecility
That raked me out of the grave. By the way, Mother:
Keep my secret: don't tell the old man I'm dead.
I want to tease him awhile."

                                        Reine had been swaying
Dizzily in the storm of his mind and the smell of death,
and far down underfoot
The swords of the low sun whirled slowly in the sea-haze
in the gorge-throat: she felt her blood
Drain from her brain, and darkness from the sides glide

7

Over her eyes; she bit her lip hard, the pain
To fight the faintness, but her nerves could not feel
What her teeth did; she slid along the rock fence,
Dislodging a stone which rolled into the canyon-depth;
She slid to her knees and fell forward, but propped herself
From the earth with her hands.

 Her son stood quietly
Observing her, then the girl Hazel ran from the house,
And raged at him with her eyes, leaning to help, but Reine
Shook her head against the dimness, and rose
Unhelped, and stood. Her thin face framed in the sorrel
 hair
Was suddenly very beautiful, chalk white emblazoned
With intensely blue eyes and the bright blood-lace
On the bitten lip. She attempted to speak and failed,
And sucked breath and said carefully, "It is not true.
You are sick, I think. Nobody ever has come
Back from . . ." "Sht!" he said, "keep my secret.
The girl is here." She turned and stared: "Oh, Hazel?
 Stay with me.
He pretends that he's dead. People don't walk and . . .
Breathe . . ." She began to tremble violently, her hands
 and mouth.
She said, "Please, dear. Please, dear," and then shrilly:
 "Go back!
Go to your place and lie down and be quiet, pull the clay
 over you,
I can't endure this." He said, "All right. I'll tell her then.
I was killed on Meserole Island twenty days ago.
I lay in the shade and watched myself swell
Until they found me and buried me, but after that

8

I got so angry lying in the dark remembering, I poured
    my soul
With sickening pain into my body again,
And more or less fixed up the rotten tissues, and broke
The choking earth. Only don't tell my father Bull Gore.
I want to play wi' that bull."

                        When Gore came home
It was a little after midnight; Hoult had closed himself
In the room that he used to use, and Reine feigned sleep,
Her weeping face to the wall. Gore lay down beside her
In ignorance that his son lay in the house.
In the morning Reine washed herself and went to Hoult's
    room;
He was not there. She gasped and ran downstairs
To the room off the kitchen: "Hazel, where is he?
Where has he gone?" The girl, her thin dark face
Drowned in sleep and the oily hair, moaned "No,"
And sat up in bed, rounding her mouth to scream,
Remembering fear; Reine saw the black eyes of her breasts
And the black O of her mouth, three points of a triangle
In the gray swimming light, a long round scream
Came from the apex. Reine said, "What, have you seen
    him?"
It screamed again; Reine shook the lean shoulder, claw-
    ing in
Under the ridge of the scapula, and looked at the dim
    face and said,
"Nothing but sleep." She ran barefoot outdoors,
Her thin shift fallen from one shoulder, looking for Hoult,
    but summer cloud
Covered the mountain; nothing beyond the house-yard

Could be seen in the curded half-light. She circled the
    house
And met Gore in the doorway, half-dressed, his black-
    haired
Chest and belly bulging from the belted trousers. He said,
    "What the devil?
What is the yelling?" Reine said, "Hoult was here
Last night, he's gone." "Who was here?" "Hoult," she
    said bitterly.
"Have you forgotten him? You had a son named Hoult.
You have no son. He came home last night, or his angry
    ghost,
To say that he was killed on that bloody island."
"You are talking nonsense," he said. "What island?"
    under heavy brows
Observing the girl Hazel, who had come shuddering,
    slightly enclothed
In a blanket from her bed; dark though she was,
Her feet were as white as Reine's; he said, "For Christ'
    sake,
What is she talking about?" She opened her mouth quite
    round on silence. Reine said,
"You sent him there, though I begged you on my knees.
    Meserole Island:
Is that a place? He was only seventeen.
I prayed to you and to him, but you'd hypnotized him:
    your insane talk
About courage and honor." Gore shook his head on the
    thick throat, like an animal
When the blood blinds it. He said, "O God, talk sense.
Did you think you saw him?" She stiffened herself erect,
With lidless eyes, the blue-staring irises

10

White-ringed in the blind whites. "Saw him. And touched,
      heard," she said, "smelled
The smell of death. Now he's gone back there.
That is what we have sons for." He said to the girl: "You.
Did *you* see him?" Reine, suddenly weeping, embraced
      him,
Hiding her face on the black moss of his breast.
"You loved him too." He said, "Did *you* see him, Hazel?"
"Uh," she said, "yes." He said, "If you both saw him,
Then Hoult was here." Reine leaning against him felt his
      thick body
Tremble like a tall rock down on the shore
When winter seas pound the cliff.

                              Gore went outdoors
After a time, and returned. "You make me sick.
He's taken a horse and saddle and gone for a ride, and
      taken a rest
From screaming women. Get me some breakfast." Later
      in the morning
He was back and forth between the barn and corral
Several times, eyeing the ridges; for the cloud had lifted
Toward the top of the mountain, its dark-gray belly still
      contained the peaks;
The two ranch-dogs, bleak old Sport and his pup,
Walked by his knees, the younger lifted her head
And pointed; Gore looked that way and saw nothing
But the heavy ridges plunging to slate-blue sea; he heard
      the air
Ripped at his side, and on the instant the rough-edged
Voice of a rifle and its echo. The young shepherd-bitch
Was hit and screaming. Gore stared at the rifle's voice
And saw the mounted marksman far down the ridge-drive.

11

He shouted at him, recognizing his own bay horse,
And turned to look to the dog. Her hindquarters
Seemed to be dead; she was propped on her forelegs,
Bleeding from throat and back, but in a moment
Fell over on her side. He had his hand on her
And she was choking; he saw the bay fetlocks
And heard Hoult's voice: "Hello, Dad. Good shot: ah?
I thought it was a coyote." Gore stared up at him,
Sitting without expression, corpse-faced and war-clad on
      the bay horse, and said bitterly,
"You thought *what?* Let it be. How are you, Hoult?
The poor thing's dying." Meanwhile the older dog,
His hackles and his back bristling, slunk half a circle
Behind the heels of the horse and sprang at Hoult's thigh,
Hooked his teeth in and hung; the horse leaped sidewise;
      cloth and flesh tore,
But Hoult seemed to feel nothing; and the dog fled,
Head down, slavering big flakes of foam; he avoided
      Reine,
Who was coming from the house. Gore meanwhile: "Watch
      out!
Hell, did he cut you?" Hoult savagely checked the horse
And said, "The cloth is rotten, so is the flesh." He looked
      down and said,
"So is the blood. You were out last night when I came
      home. Did you
And your old buddies decide what the war's about?
I came to ask. You were all for it, you know;
And keeping safe away from it, so to speak, maybe you see
Reasons that we who only die in it can't."
He said carefully, "We had a captain that gave lectures,
But he was such a liar." Gore looked at him

In silence; the greenish drab leather of Hoult's face
Hanging loose on the bones looked dreadfully
Like a mirror of his mind; and Hoult said to his mother,
Who had come, white and thin, staring alternately
At Hoult and the shot dog, which moaned and snapped
In her last pain—he said, "He's dumb, he won't talk.
I asked him a decent question: by God he'll *sing*
Before I've done." Gore with some dignity,
Swallowing the dark-veined anger that swelled his throat,
Stood up and said, "Her pain is over. Hoult, you look sick.
Y' look pretty bad. Y' been in hospital?" "Yea?" he said.
     "No:
A little deeper." Reine shrilly interposed her voice between
     them:
"Where did you ride to, dear? You frightened me,
Going off so early." He said, "To see a friend. Ah?
Your friend young Larson. We're going deer-hunting.
That's why I'm testing out the old thirty-thirty: it's no
     Garand
But it'll do. Y' ought to 'a' seen him turn red and pale
When I mentioned you. By God, there, you too
Waving the same colors! These blonds are bad liars, Dad.
You must 'a' noticed, they have flags in their cheeks.
But dark men like you and me, dark thick-skinned men
Can lie the world into hell as naturally
As babies breathe." He swung himself from the saddle
And fell on hands and knees, groaning. Gore caught the
     reins, Reine cried,
"Oh, Hoult, Hoult, what's the matter?" He labored stiffly
And stood himself on his feet, propped on the rifle-butt,
     saying,
"It is the pain. D'y' think it costs nothing

13

To make decayed flesh work?" She saw the discolored
Blood on his thigh, brown and thin, clot and serum,
And through the split cloth the wound, but for very weari-
ness
Stared and said nothing. He answered and said, "*Dogs
have no teeth.
But I could show you something under my shirt—
I will, some time. By the way, where do you keep the
cartridges?" He saw his father
Leading the horse toward the corral, and called: "Hey,
Dad.
Where do you keep the shells for the rifle?
I could only find four." Gore stopped and gazed at him,
And said, "That's all." "Ha?" he said. Reine said, "You
can't
Buy them now, dear; it's all for the Army. Hoult . . .
Hoult dear . . ." She laid her hand on his arm: "Be good
to your father.
He has been patient today, and I believe
He loves you deeply. And if he edged you
Into that horror, it wasn't for lack of love, but what he
thought
Honorable and right; and he himself
Went in the other war, and would again if they'd take him.
And remember,
You were eager to go. I went on my knees to you,
If you remember, and prayed you with tears
To stay home, but you wouldn't." "I've paid for it,"
He said, "he'll pay. What's the matter with you, Mother?
Is he worn out?" She did not answer, and he said,
"Women must have it, I understand: can't he provide it?

14

Is he impotent?" "No, Hoult." "And you're still fond of
      him: how dare you
Cheat him wi' that blond kite?" She said, "It's not true.
      Hoult, your mind:
Something has happened to it." "Yea," he said, "why not?
But it still works. Oh, Mother: a haggard old woman
With a boy her son's age. You might 'a' looked in the
      mirror: although your hair
And teeth are young still: your face is as dry and bloodless
As a dead moon." She said, "This is a dirty dream
That you dreamed underground. I do not think
You believe it yourself; I think you hate
Everyone you ever knew." He said, "Why not?
And several others. Ah, today's Sunday, people are in
      church, I believe, praying God
To bless their enemies: that is burn 'em alive and blast 'em
To a bloody mash: tomorrow is Monday the thirty-first;
      Tuesday
Is the first day of deer-season." He had counted the days
On his fingers like an eager child; she laid her hand
On his joined hands: "Is it because you hate
Even the little brown deer? Oh, Hoult, your hands!
You are burning up with fever!" "Sure," he said, "de-
      composition's
A kind of fever. Rotten wood shines in the dark.
Rotten hay-ricks catch fire. Rotten countries make war.
      Rotten old women
Seduce boys. Did you get him drunk first?" She answered
      slowly,
"It would be better if you'd go back to that island grave.
There's nothing here."

                    Gore returning from the paddock,

She was silent. Hoult said to her, "Did y' read 'n the
        papers
About V-1? *Verjeltungswaf*," he pronounced it English,
"Retaliation-weapon. Those intelligent hyenas
Have probably got more Vs in the shop: *mine's* called
        V-X,
What I'm here for. It flies in the air and goes boom.
        Watch it." He grinned at his father,
Who said uneasily, "How long is your furlough, Hoult?
Ten days?" "Yea, thirty days." "Fine," he said. "Well,
Let's go down to the house. I see you've earned
A pair of chevrons. That's fine." "Yea," he answered,
"I stole these clothes."
                        Old Moro Soto
Stood by the door silently eyeing them, and stood aside
While they went in. Reine returned in a moment
And called to him: "Where is Hazel?" He looked down
        and said,
"Jesus, she gone." "She's gone? Where has she gone?"
"She say she afraid of here, she going walk home
To her own people." Reine said, "Oh. She'll have
Quite a walk. And then talk all night. Listen, Moro:
What she thinks is not true. My son is sick
And has a fever: the rest is foolishness.
People don't . . . you know what. Nobody now believes
That even Christ did. Go up and bury poor Rosie, will
        you?
She was a good dog, she was killed by accident."
He said, "Sport he gone too." "Oh, they are thinning
        out," she said,
"They're thinning out."

                        16

While Hoult and his father in
the long living-room
Made words together, Gore said he believed that the Ger-
man war
Would be over in two months. "They'll fight in France,
But as soon as you come to the German border
They quit: they lie down on their backs and beg: and I
hope to God
We'll have no mercy." Hoult said, "Why?" He stared and
answered,
"Then we'll bomb hell out of Tokyo." Hoult said, "We've
nothing
To avenge on Germany; and not so much on the Japs as
they have on us. Poor little dogs, trying
To act like white men. So why so fierce?" Gore gaped at
him
And heard a thin, gritty and whining noise, his teeth
Grinding together behind the calmly said words and dark
wooden face; and sudden white foam
Shot the brown lips. He said, "My God, Hoult, what?"
Hoult shook his head
And attempted to speak, and said, "Nothing," and said,
"Have you ever seen a flame-thrower? No, I suppose,
Not in your time. We roast them, you know, screaming,
in their little nests. That was my occupation
For a time. But now I'm thinking of being a preacher, I
got religion.
Under fire, you know." Reine came in and he glanced at
her,
And said, "I'll go around and preach to the people: For
Christ' sake amen. We must build gibbets
On every mountain-peak and every high hill,

17

All along the sky-line conspicuous gibbets, and if any
    person
Begins to say we have to save England or rescue France
    or avenge the Jews—take him up and hang him,
He is pimping for war. If he says democracy,
Remember they pimped for war and they will again—
    take him up and hang him. Or if he says we must
    save
Civilization: they said it: take them up and hang them.
    If they say, My country,
Right or wrong—they are pimping for war, take them
    up and hang them.
Higher than Haman. Hell, we'll have a fine orchard
When the sun ripes the plums."

                                    Reine listened to him,
And thought she was too exhausted to intervene. There
    was nothing. She went to the southward
Window, and set her face to the glass,
And gazed down the harsh gorge-bank to the dark sea,
    where it stood
Like water in a well. The sun on her autumn-leaf hair
Made a light in the room, and she heard Hoult:
"You'll be there, old man, right along with the President
And his paid mouths; and the radio-shouters, the writers,
    the world-planners, the heavy bishops,
The England-lovers, the little poets and college profes-
    sors,
The seducers of boys, the pimps of death, the pimps:
    Ahh—
Stretched pimps all in a row,
Swing high, swing low,

Swing high in the mountain wind; and the birds perch,
and the black tongues
Loll on their chins. Oh, we'll have wars yet, but not for
nothing,
Not like this one for nothing."
Gore controlled
The wrath that gorged his broad throat. He came close
to Hoult
And overhung him like a dark rock and said: "I take it
you've
Obeyed orders and served, fought and cracked up.
You've done your duty. I hope you'll come to yourself
After you've rested. We'll let this pass." He turned
Heavily toward the door and went out, Hoult stammering
behind him,
"Ah, just a minute, a minute," and Reine heard him
Leap up and stand. She heard the breath sob in his teeth.
After a time he said hoarsely, "You can't imagine
How hard it was to pull down the rifle's eye
From the man to the dog. Why does your hair shine so?
What have you done?" She turned and he had come close
to her,
And said, "Your eyes don't shine. Oh, it is horrible
To hate, and hate, and hate, and go over their reasons
again,
And they had no reason to condemn me to death
Because a German dog hoped to steal something
From a Russian dog. I know: I read his book: while we
rotted
In Scofield barracks: and we were sold to death
By liars and fools. Now there is nothing left
But to envy and degrade life with our stinking bodies

And betrayed minds. I might have had joy and freedom, and someone
    and someone
As beautiful as you, Mother, and loved her, even
If she were false as you. If she were still kind,
Who cares, who cares? But they pushed me down
Out of the sunlight, out of the decent air into dirt and
    darkness: and I fought back,
I am only a bitter will holding up a corpse
That walks and hates: even you, Mother,
Wish I were back under the damned white crosses
Between the bush and the sea." "No, Hoult." "Be careful.
I am degradation and death." She said, "No, Hoult. Life
Is what degrades." "Ah?" he said. "I wouldn't know.
They stole my life. I think it might have flowed clean
Even to the floor of the cup. My death's not clean. This
    is it: Ah,
I haven't told you the half. I was put down
And shovelled under: *you* know: gypped, shipped and
    killed,
Like others, dug in and finished. I was nearly asleep,
Nearly dissolved in the rank flesh of the island: I saw your
    face
Leaning over me like a little thin moon
In that black sky. God, how I hated you." She gasped:
    "*I* am not the one
That sent you there." "And loved you," he said. "Hate-
    love, death-life, *you* know:
Amphibian. That was the spark: without that
This run-down engine would have . . . run down . . .
    They caught me young, you know,
I'd never known any woman, and the army sea-gulls

20

Are things to puke at. Gypped, ah? Gypped again.
    Gypped out of everything.
Even the quietness and sleep of death, the common black
    orchid
That blossoms for dogs and cats, lizards and birds,
When life grows too foul to bear: gypped out of that too.
    So I lay choking, and the red rage
Spread up and sprouted, clawed me out. You are beauti-
    ful, Mother.
I didn't know you were beautiful. I
Am evil, I think, an offense against Nature, an evil will
Bearing up a corpse: will you put your arms around me
And kiss me? I am lonely in pain." She, instinctively
Retreating from him, had felt her shoulder-blades
Press the glass of the window; but now she did
What he desired, her mouth dry as dead leaves
On his throat's raging pulse. He was not like a son,
But like a man. She strove against him and said,
"Let me go. Ah. Ah. No," twisting her body
Aside from him; he held her and said, "I told you
I am degradation." But the dead are a feeble race.
She turned her little wrist-bones against his throat
And broke free and stood clear. Coldly, and it seemed
Slowly, she thought that in a world grown monstrous,
    rabies-bitten
And nightmare-false, where millions of men are sacrificed
For no reason but vanity, thousands of ships and great
        fleets of planes with crammed wombs day and night
Labor over farthest oceans to debark death, not on armies
        only,
But old women, babies and little dogs; and worse is con-
        nived at, and worse is coming: if in such a world

21

A tortured boy wants anything: though it were vicious
Two years ago, it has no color now, and why
Had she denied him? Disgust?—is not a presentable
Cause to be cruel.
                Hoult stood, panting hard, but his
       wooden face
Had no expression and stared at her. At length he said,
"There was a fellow in the Bible who said he wouldn't
Believe until he'd laid his hand in the wounds.
Okay: do so." He tore off the soiled tunic
And dragged his shirt up from the belt, and bared
His chest's left side. It was black with wounds, and one
Like a wide-grinning mouth, where a mortar-shell frag-
       ment
Had crushed in through two ribs, and enmawed itself
In the lung's room. Reine whined in her throat and stood
With shut eyes, tottering; her hand clutched her left
       breast
As if all the pain were there. Hoult said, "You weak leaf,
Can't you even look?" She fluttered her eyelids as if they
       squinted
At the sun in his glory; and then wide open
White-ringed stood staring. He said, "All right: put in.
Put in your hand and believe." She whispered, "I believe.
Have mercy on me." "Damn you, put in your hand."
She came like a sleepwalker feeling her way,
Wide sightless eyes, and laid her hand on the purulent
Lips of the wound. He said, "Deeper," she slipped
Her hand into the hollow, this lung was gone, she felt the
       dreadful
Fever of his body, and the heart flapping and leaping
In its wet sheaths, and the shudder of the diaphragm.

22

He breathed like a running dog, saying, "Deeper, deeper.
        Oh,
You're near me now. Oh, I've been lonely.
Cut off by infinite hate and the foulness of death
From all that live.—Draw it out, dear. The pain.
Oh," he gasped, "out!" She felt his heart clench and
        strangle, and hastily
Dragging her hand away, the jag end and splinter
Of a rib scored it, her own blood in a moment
Mixed with the bloody exudate. Hoult said, "Pain, pain.
But not this horror," handling the base of his throat
On the left side; and they heard Bolivar Gore
Come to the room and come in, saying, "Hazel's run out
        on us
For some reason—" He looked at his wife and son
And was silent. Hoult's shirt had fallen into place
Over the wounds, and he groaned and said: "Old dog, you
        smell something?
Put up your nose and bay, but you'll never know
What we were doing here." Gore eyed them heavily under
        dark brows. Reine faltered: "He was showing me
His wounds. I mean his wounds." Gore said, "I see. Yes.
        The girl has made off
For some reason. I've fixed up the fire again: you'll have
        to finish
Fixing the meat." She gazed at her right hand, varnished
        with blood and slime, and whispered,
"With this." Gore said, "My God, what's that? Changing
        a bandage?
Is the wound running?" And to Hoult: "You ought to
        be in hospital.

23

Let me look at it." Hoult said, "Oh, no, you don't. Nor
   no hospital.
I quit the Army. I thought I'd probably be . . . killed:
So I deserted." Gore said, "You what?" Reine jerked her
   head up
From seeing for the first time the infection-drenched
Cut on the back of her hand, and wondering how soon
It might catch fire. Hoult said, "I deserted.
Under fire, you know; in the face of the enemy.
I didn't want to get killed. Will you hide me
When they come after me?" Gore stood silent, the lines
In his face deepening to sooty slashes; Hoult smiled
   faintly, and Reine
Remembered he'd never smiled since he came home
Until this moment. She sighed and looked again at the
   scratch on her hand, and answered, "He's lying
Just to torment you. You're easily teased, Bull." Hoult
   said: "Father . . .
You are my father . . . I'm safe here, you'll hide and
   save me. I might even be shot, you know. This is
   not Germany,
Where they say sons and fathers run to the Gestapo
To inform on each other: this is liberal America, where
   blood is still
Thicker than government." Gore looked down at his wrist-
   watch, his hand so shaking that he was unable
To read the dial; he said hoarsely, "I will give you
Twenty-four hours." "Before you rat on me," Hoult said.
"You'll be well cut in the interval. It seems I've found
   something
To cut you with." He changed and said, "O God,
How heartless you are! What? Your own son?

24

Father, have mercy on me, I can't believe
You'd betray your own son. Besides that now
I'm listed missing, but if they court-martial me,
Think what a shame and disgrace to *you*, as well
As death to *me*. Have mercy on yourself and me.
You had such a grand record in the other war: weren't
        you promoted
Sergeant or something? And though you never saw fight,
Still you *did* land in France, where General Patton, Per-
        shing, I mean,
Is hacking them into pieces like a hot hawk
In a panic of pigeons— All right, all right: no mercy.
I'll make a bargain: tell me one decent reason
Why the United States got into this war,
I'll go and give myself up. I'll give you"—he mocked him,
        pretending
To peer at a little watch on a shaking wrist—"twenty-
        four hours
To find one reason. Don't say Pearl Harbor though.
That was a trick, a dirty one. They had duped us
Deep into war, they'd fooled us into doing everything
Except declare it and send armies abroad: but if we were
        blooded,
We'd be mad enough. Germany wouldn't attack
Although we sank her boats and supplied her enemies:
They needled the touchy Japs and they did it for them.
        And don't, for God's sake,
Pretend that we had to fight while we still had friends
In Europe: what do we want of Europe? We're stronger
        than the whole rats' nest
This side of Russia, those that fight and those that lie
        down, and you knew it,

25

And it's now proved. Oh, Oh," he moaned, "God damn
    you, haven't you
One single reason? And I died for that? Nor don't say
    freedom:
War's freedom's killer. Don't say freedom for foreigners,
Unless you intend to kill Russia on top of Germany and
    Britain on Japan, and churn the whole world
Into one bloody bubble-bath; don't say democracy;
Don't talk that mush. And don't pretend that the world
Will be improved, or good will earned, or peace
Made perfect by blasting cities and nations into bloody
    choppets: if you believe *that*
You'll believe anything. There are lockable madhouses
For fools to simper and howl in: well, the whole planet's
    one,
And here you're locked. You will not trouble the moons
    of Jupiter, nor the sweet planets that dance
To the piping of the suns in Orion's belt.—I'm going up
    to my room, Mother,
And groan awhile. If you fix any food,
Fetch me up a plate. This wrecked machine, this hurting
And rotting resurrection has to be fuelled: the bitter will
That runs it is something else again."

                 He was going out, staggering
With shrill exhaustion, handling his way
Between the table and the wall. Gore said, "Wait a minute,
Here's something for you," and relaxed his clenched fists;
    Reine instantly
Began to cry like a gull, "Ah Ah Ah Ah," Gore through
    that swarm
And wind of wailing, lightly as he thought, tapped
Hoult's jaw with his open palm; lightly, but Hoult

Fell across the doorway like grass from a scythe, his head
Against the foot of the jamb. Gore stood over him, saying
"Don't talk against your country. Don't do it." Reine
        had stopped crying,
And stood and stared; and at length Hoult's hand
Crept on the floor, dragging back toward the shoulder
In the first effort to rise: it was then Gore pitied him
And knelt beside him. "Damn it, I'm sorry, boy.
I didn't mean to hit hard." But Reine: her timing was
        strange:
She had cried before the blow and been silent after, and
        now
It was repented she avenged it, hammering Gore's back
With her small fists. Gore, without noticing her:
"I kind of lost my temper. Ah . . . forgive me, son.
I know you're not quite right in your mind: it'll pass.
Battle-fatigue. What the hell, boy, thumbs up.
I'll stick by you." Hoult crawled on the floor and hauled
        himself
Up by the door-post. Brown blood ran on his brow, and
        he said painfully:
"You needn't be sorry for me: I and you
Will have a settling.
Be sorry for the decent and loyal people of America,
Caught by their own loyalty, fouled, gouged and bled
To feed the power-hunger of politicians and make trick
        fortunes
For swindlers and collaborators. For a time's coming—
Fairly soon, you'll not see it—when the ends of the earth,
        from east and west one world, will close on your
        country

27

Like the jaws of a trap; but people will say, Be quiet, we
       were fooled before. We know that all governments
Are thugs and liars, let them fight their own battles: and
       the trap is closing, and an angry spirit
Will go through the camps whispering mutiny in con-
       scripts' ears: your rulers are cooking another
       world-war,
Come and we'll kill them: and that spirit will be *mine*. It
       will scream like an eagle
Over the mountains, over the quisling cities and burning
       cities and sabotaged air-fields—while the enemy
Makes good his beach-heads. But who knows that sub-
       mission
Is better than war? *I* don't, *I* don't. I read Tolstoy too:
His little gospels: a fellow had them
And cut his throat the night before embarkation: if we
       were Christian
It would be easy answers, but we're not Christian.
I am the resurrection and the *death*, ha?—I'm going
       upstairs:
Keep your paws off me."

                Late the next day
Reine saw a moving point far down the gorge-road, and
       anxiously
Watched it; any new thing made her anxious now.
When it came out again from behind the woods
It was a horseman; she knew the color of the horse.
At length he approached the house, but went to the pad-
       dock instead
And returned walking, carrying a saddle-bag
And a hunting-carbine. Reine, amazed, waited for him

By the great calla lilies that live in the leakage
Under the stilted water-tank: "Darling, what is it?
Have you come *here?*" "What?" he said. "Yes, Hoult
     asked me.
Didn't he tell you?" They spoke low and stood carefully
Well apart from each other, and Reine said wearily, "He
     said
You were going hunting." "He asked me to come to sup-
     per and sleep here;
He wants to start before daylight. He's . . . he insisted.
Is he better now?" Reine said, "I'm . . . terrified.
I love Hoult." "Ye'," Larson said, "he's changed, he's
     been
Through hell I guess. I had no craving
To kill deer at this time." "Oh, David," she said, "be
     careful. I mean
Take care of him." She laughed feebly. "You'll get
Practically nothing to eat, the girl has gone,
And I can't cook." "I can, I'll help you." They heard a
     distant
Creaking of saddle leather. Reine unconsciously
Stopped breathing and looked sidelong: it was Bull Gore
Riding toward the corral. Larson said, "I forgot.
I've got your mail; it was in the box when I came by."
     He gave her a paper
And two letters; she, without looking at them,
Said hastily: "I have to tell you: he is . . . not . . .
Like people are. He is . . . as if he were not living
And had come back."
     Gore came behind them; he had turned
From the corral when he saw them and ridden down.
Reine turned her tormented face to him and said,

29

"It's David Larson; Hoult asked him." Gore said, "How
    are you?" and Reine
In her anxiety let the foldings of paper
Fall from her hand. Larson gathered them up. Reine said,
"He brought the mail from the box. Here." Gore an-
    swered,
"Hoult can't go hunting, he's sick," and ripped open
One of the envelopes; yellow paper, a telegram
Mailed from the Monterey office; while he read, it shook
Without a wind. He read again and said furiously,
"The bastards." Reine said, "Oh, what?" He reached it
    toward her,
His horse excited by his emotion leaped sidewise
From the fluttered paper. Gore checked him savagely and
    said, "The bastards,"
And gave the paper to Reine: the usual fatal formula,
". . . Your son Hoult Gore . . ." Reine said, "Deeply
    regret!
Stuffed shirts!" She folded the paper on the creases and
    said,
"I'll give it to Hoult," but jerked it flat again
And handed it to Dave Larson. Gore said savagely,
"Give it here." He snatched it, wheeled short, and ran his
    horse
Up the hill to the paddock.

      Reine said, "Hoult's watching us,
Behind that window, I saw him move.
We must go in at once. Now remember what he was
When you knew him: strong and big-shouldered though
    still a boy, and sweet-natured,
But even then he was always reading and thinking; I
    think he might've been a great . . . scientist

If he'd had . . . time. Remember him

As he used to . . ." She came to the door and went in,
    and Larson

Looked once over his shoulder at the white clouds

And warm hills and went in.

                                Hoult said, "Did she tell
    you all? What was she telling you?" Reine hastily:

"About Hazel going out. He says he'll help me get sup-
    per." "Yea?" he answered,

"Did she tell you I'm dead? It's true.

But th' dead have eyes." Reine sharply sighed: "I've got
    it started: if there's enough. You forgot, Hoult,
    to tell me

You'd asked a guest." "What," he said, "was that paper

You handed around? Let *him* talk." "Why," Larson said,
    "a . . . letter, I brought the letters

From the mail-box . . ." Reine said, "It was a—false—

Telegram. Deeply regrets: how do they dare to be

Stuffed shirts over dead boys?" He answered, "You
    looked ridiculous

Handing it from hand to hand: I thought at least

The Atlantic Charter: you looked ridiculous. How are
    you making out, Mother,

Between the bull and the calf? All smooth and shameless?"

        "Hoult. Please!" and she said to Larson, "A
        horrible

Dream that he has . . ." Hoult said, "Do you dare to
    make love to him before my face? Well . . . pa-
    tience awhile.

She's right: I dream all the time: I was dreaming

About three dead men." She, her voice torn and thin:
        "What do you mean?" He said,

31

"And a live woman." She turned to Larson, and breathed,
        and ruled herself and said steadily: "He is not fit
To see you. You'd better go." Hoult said, "What? No.
Buddies of mine. Hake Newton from Pennsylvania's here
        at the moment. He was shot through the head
Before we beached. There he stands: can't you see him?"

Old Soto came in the door, hoping for supper, and they
        were so wrought
They stared at him. Hoult said, "Hake and I have great
        arguments
About—what do you think?—human dignity. He thinks
        the war
Is fought for human dignity; he thinks he gave
His life for that. Pitiful guy, ah? He went to college.
That's where they cheat them, that's where they feed on
        false fruit. A lion has dignity,
So has a hawk; even a barnyard bull or common whipped
        horse has a kind of grace: but these
Peeled apes teetering on their back legs,
Male and female,
Snickering with little shames, pleasures and wisecracks,
Or howling horror: and two billion of them:
As for that, no. And take notice, their minds are as
        ludicrous
As their bodies and societies. Human dignity? How about
        it, Hake? But people *could*
Be decent. Honest and kind; honest and kind. And free:
        people *could*
Refuse to be governed and refuse to make war.
Or couldn't they?"

                    Gore heavily came in, Hoult said,

32

"Here's the other member. What do you think, Father,
About the dignity of man? I have a friend, poor devil,
Who thinks he died for it. *I* claim it has no existence.
Man, the eventual hell of life, the animal
Toward which all evolution toiled and was damned
From the beginning. You'd better see about supper,
　　　Mother,
The boys are hungry." She looked from face to face,
Smiling with terror, and went out. Larson made to follow
　　　her, Hoult said, "Stay here.
It's woman's work. Have y'ever thought what a treasure
A good woman is? You have a mother, Dave,
And though she's not very beautiful, she is to you. How
　　　would you like it if she went dirty
And took a lover? Hell, any woman can get a lover.
The things I've seen in the Army. You and I are lucky,
　　　Dave,
We know we can sail to the tag end and tail of the world,
　　　to hell or the Marianas Islands,
And when we come home we shall find our mothers
Faithful, loving and pure. Whatever is taken from us,
That remains ours. Or if we grow cynical
And sneer at the human race: that still is ours, that star-
　　　like
Purity, that love, that religion." While he spoke he
　　　watched him
With his dead lustreless eyes; which Larson met
And looked away from, and resolutely engaged again but
　　　his feet shifted, lips thinned,
His hands fiddled and clinched. "I've noticed in the
　　　Army,"
Hoult said, "the camps are sticky with morose men

Who know what their wives are doing while they're away,
    but no one
Mistrusts his mother. Is it hot in here? Take off your coat,
    Dave,
I see you're sweating." "I?" he said hoarsely,
"No, not a bit." "Oh, yes, you are. Your forehead
Is all rashed with clear drops. Ha? Though tongues lie,
Sweat tells the truth. That's the point, you see.
Sweat is involuntary, tongues wag at will. The will
Is the corrupter. Or don't you think so?" Larson's throat
Clicked twice in the effort to swallow, and after a moment
Frail-voiced he said: "You're too deep for me, Hoult. I've
    no idea
What you're talking about." "It doesn't matter, it doesn't
    matter. You know, I can hardly wait
To hear the hawks of dawn whistle on the mountain.
    You'd think I'd seen enough killing
Where I come from: by God, I can hardly wait
To kill a buck, a young buck."
          Gore said heavily, "Yea. Tomorrow's the day
Of guns and fools. Tomorrow's the day
A cow can't walk through a bush without being shot. The
    young fools are drafted,
It'll be old ones. How much longer, Larson, d'you think
You can keep out of uniform, ah? I hear your brother
Was hurt on the Anzio beach: what does he think of you
Sitting home on your arse on an agricultural exemption?"
    Hoult answered for him:
"Right, it's the day of guns: rifle and carbine, field and
    machine and tommy, mortar and howitzer,
The great big cats and the little kitties,
The day of guns and fools. D'y'know what follows it?

34

The night of knives. That's for you civilians
To hold in your happy minds." Reine came in; Hoult,
    carefully
Avoiding her anxious gaze, turned and went out
Onto the porch.

                Several figures of shadow were standing
    there; Hoult looked beyond them
At the deep-hearted west; low crimson, soaring smoked
    amber and high rose of sundown; one of the
    shadows
Came in between and stood swaying. Hoult said, "You,
    Schultzie? You got it too?" It whispered like a
    wind and said,
"Those God-damn cocoanut palms." "Well," he said, "I'm
    sorry." The figures whispered together; Hoult
    gazed
At the deep-hearted west. Reine came to the door:
"Will you come, dear? It's ready." "What?" he said. "Oh.
    I'd nearly forgot the filth and sailed out into that
Unhuman heaven. Look at it. Think of the little rats on
    the ocean islands biting each other
Under that banner, that pure glory. It's heart-breaking.
    These boys here, Mother,
Are deceased dog-faces, friends of mine. Good fellows in
    their time, fooled out of life like me
By scoundrels and cullions. They come to watch us,
Because—as a matter of fact—I am the only dead body
    that has had the energy to get up again
Since Jesus Christ. His whip was love, they say. Mine"—
He followed her in through the door—"fury."

                He went to his father:
"Let me see the death-notice, will you? Everybody

35

But me has seen it: after all it's *my* death."
Gore said, "They told you, did they? The son of a bitch
Tally-man ought to be shot." He fished his pocket
And gave it to him. Hoult reading it held the paper
For one behind him to see. "Here, Schultz. In a week or
　　　　two
Your people up in Grant's Pass will get one. They fall
　　　　like snow
Over the country, silent and soft as snow,
Freezing the hearts they light on. And not one voice, not
　　　　one,
Curses the damned deliberate liars and dogs
That duped us in.—Have y' got a pencil?"
He said to his father, who stared and said, "Over there
In the desk. Why?"
　　　　　　　　　Reine meanwhile
Went around the table setting plates of food
At the five places; she carefully avoided
Passing behind her son, where the all but visible
Shadows were gathered. Her hands were shaking, her
　　　　blade-thin
Face was mask pale with terrified sky-blue eyes,
And her mouth lined with lipstick. Hoult went to the old
Roller-top desk where Gore kept his accounts,
And sitting by it made a quick drawing
On the telegram back. Reine said, "Please, Hoult,
Come while it's hot." He found a match in the desk,
　　　　dipped its butt in ink,
And overtraced the pale pencil lines; there was red ink,
　　　　which with his finger-tip
He streaked on for near sea and far sky, and glanced at
　　　　the attentive shades

36

Behind his shoulder: "Ha? Right?" He stood up and said,
    "Yeh, very comical."
                        Gore gently said, "For Christ' sake
Come and sit down." Hoult laid the paper before him and
    said,
"The boys like comics," and went to his place and sat
    and wolfed food. Gore gazed at the drawing: the
    low foreshore
Of a sea island: on the far ridge three cocoanut palms in
    the red-ink sky, on the near strand
A great set rat-trap, wooden base and wire jaw: and the
    beauty
Of a drawing is in the lines, each line was beautiful
By itself and with the others. There were only a dozen
    lines. Gore said, "Pretty good. Why comic?"
    Hoult swallowed
His lump of meat and said hoarsely, "Because the trap
    has no bait. There was no reason." Gore sighed
    and said,
"I am not laughing." Hoult said, "The boys did. Well,
    it's not finished, I'll finish
After I eat." He took it from his father and reached it
Across the vacant place to Larson, who looked,
And gave it to Reine. Then Gore and the others for the
    first time
Became aware of the vacant place at the table; Gore stood
    up and said,
"Where is old Soto?" Reine, her thin face, raddled mouth,
Staring blue eyes, answered: "Gone after Hazel.
One by one, one by one." Gore said, "The hell he has,"
And left the room. They heard him calling
In the house and outdoors. He returned and said,

37

"The old fool. Horse and all."

Hoult meanwhile

Finished his picture; he put a little man, neck and
    shoulder
Under the clapper of the rat-trap; he scraped a match-
    end
In the neck of the catsup bottle to make a blood-splatch
From the manikin's mouth. The tomato red
And pale smears of red ink, their insane relation
Made the drawing an obscenity; and out the west window
The darkening sky over the foundered sun
Wore the same colors, acid pink and foul spot,
As if the indecent mind of man had infected
The endless Pacific sky: but that's not possible:—or is it?

Hoult laid his picture

On a clear place on the table, he did not show it
To his ghosts as before, but the living only, and he said:
"Now it is comic. Take it in remembrance of me. This
    is my body
That was broken for nothing. Drink it: this is my blood
That was spilled for no need. Oh, yes: for victory:
That rat-sucked hawk-egg. Next winter when a thousand
    carrier planes from sunrise to darkness day after
    day rage over Tokyo,
And Germany is a blind giant beaten to his knees, twitch-
    ing red pulp flayed in the knife-storm: which one
    of you
Will be mean enough to exult? Or decent enough to pity?
    Or alive to know? You, Mother?
I wish I knew. Oh," he said sadly, "the picture's name?
The War Department Regrets. Mother," he said,
But the room was growing dark, and Reine in terror

38

Lighting the lamps. She muttered her scarlet lips; Larson
said,
"What?" "No," she answered, "I was praying," and she
whispered audibly,
"Deliver us from evil, deliver us from evil, deliver us
From evil . . ." Gore said, "You could get one of those
prayer-wheels,
Or play it on top of the mountain on a phonograph. Lis-
ten, Hoult,"
He said heavily, "there have always been wars;
And people get killed in them;
And now there are more people, there are more killed.
So what? A decent man will fight for his country
When it's in trouble." Hoult said, "I know. No matter
how rotten
Wrong is the cause. Mother, I'd cry my eyes out for us,
but always
Fury comes first. Think of ten million—no, twenty mil-
lion—no, forty—" his mind like a tired horse
Slipping and swimming among the blood-lakes—"lives
cast away,
With all their infinite capacities, nothing used but the
modulations of torment:—for what? For nothing.
Nothing, nothing: the show. The old whirligig, the old
runaround, the old up-and-down,
And I am sick of it. You know what they call it? They
call it History. What our people came over
From stifled Europe to escape. So now we go back, hot
on the haggard whore's trail, that rouged-up, dis-
ease-blown
And lip-sticked queen—y' might 'a' rubbed some shoe-
polish into your eyelashes,

Mother, made yourself perfect—twice now we've taken
An ordinary European kennel-quarrel
And blown it into a world-war, and swollen our fate
Fat with dropsical victories, but wait a little, the third
        time's the charm, the eternal—
Not justice, what is justice?—the eternal
Retaliation—will catch. What's that to us? Be happy, for
        here are four of us, complete and childless,
That are sailing out of these things into carefree eternity.
        Tomorrow we hunt the deer, and next day
Is not our trouble. I mean *three*, I mean three."
                                Reine shuddered and said,
"What is death like?" Painful-eyed she was watching
One of the lamps; the wick was wound too high and a
        snake-tongue
Of smoke flicked up the glass, but she couldn't imagine
What was wrong nor how cure it; her strained blue gaze
Worked back and forth between that and Hoult's face:
"What is death *like?*" "What?" he said. "It's bad for
        birds. It's bad
If life is good." "You are my lord and my king," she
        answered.
"You will do what you please."
                                She felt a motion
In her lap and looked down, and saw her own hand
Crawl on the lap of her skirt over her thighs,
White in the shadow, clenching and unclenching like a
        sick spider
By its own will, not hers, and she could not stop it, she
        gasped, "Oh, Hoult!
Look here, look here." He came beside her and said,

40

"What is it doing, is it writing?" She said, "It hurts.
    Oh—Hoult: that dirty
Thing that you thought and I denied it: I lied." "I know,"
    he answered.
Her hand lay quiet, and she said, "But now I loathe him.
He is like a white slug. . . . He has a mother and a
    father." Hoult said,
"So had I. So had the boys that were killed today.
It's funny about your hand being a truth-teller: I knew
    that sweat—
I noticed an hour ago. The humble excretions: blood,
    sweat and spit, as the fellow said,
They tell the truth." Reine answered, "I am at peace.
I think I could even sleep."

            In the black throat of dawn several rifle-shots
Were heard far down the mountain along the coast-road,
    where lawless hunters had fascinated their deer
With spotlights, and sprayed them with tracer-bullets—
    for the army camps
Leaked ammunition—but under the pale gray forehead
    nearer shots crackled; men had camped overnight
At the heads of canyons, to catch their game in the first
    glimmer of the season, tame and unwatchful
After ten secure months; and when it fled up the mountain
    from the rifles below,
Here were the rifles.
                Meanwhile at the Gore ranch-house
Lamps had been lighted; Hoult and his friend rode up
    the ridge
Under the first gray streak that gleamed in the east, where
    but now Orion

41

And the dog-star had stood.

Reine lay in bed,

Stiff as a two-day corpse, and she heard the hoof-strokes,
The low voices and creaking of stirrup-leather
Die up the hill. She heard Gore come upstairs
Into the room, carrying a lamp, its light
Reddened through her shut eyelids; he said, "He's crazy,
I couldn't stop him; maybe it'll be good for him.
Hell, he's not fit to ride; I told Larson
To try and take care of him. My God, Reine,
Are you *asleep* still?" He held the lamp over her,
She clenched her eyes and her fists; he peered at her
And saw her blade-thin face quiver in the wave of her hair,
         and said,
"Y' might've got up and made coffee for them: *I* made it,
And it was rotten." While he spoke, a rifle-shot
Clapped in the mountain dawn, and Reine's whole body
Jerked on the bed as if the bullet had entered her; and
         again
She lay rigid and still. Gore said, "By God,
That's a grim kind of sleep." He went to the door and
         returned,
And said, "Are you sick? What's the matter with you?"
He laid his hand on her hip and she felt like glass, but she
         answered,
"No: resting." "Rest?" he said.

He went out

And was saddling a horse, to ride on the hill
And guard his fences; the sun came up and stood intol-
         erably bright
On the ridge of the world; and Gore saw Hoult, black in
         the light-river,

42

Returning down, hunched over the saddle-horn
Like a sick monkey. Gore called him and said, "No luck?"
      He straightened,
And answered: "One." Gore said, "Where is it?" He made
      no answer.
Gore said, "Are you all right?" and he made no answer.
      Gore followed him
Toward the house; but checked on the way, seeing smoke
On the shore in the north: cigarette or camp-fire,
Or those contraband tracer-bullets, had lighted
The foreland grass: but it was well to the north,
And the smoke spired straight up, like the stem and cap
      of an immense mushroom:
There was no wind.
               Three distant rifle-shots
Hammered in quick succession; Gore saw in his mind
      Reine's glassy body
Jerk on the bed; but when he came into the house
She'd come downstairs. She and Hoult were standing
Facing each other but far apart in the long room,
She in her white night-dress, uncombed, her hair
Matted and staring, and unwashed, for a trickle
Of dried-up blood lay from her bitten under-lip
Across the hollow of her cheek. When Gore came in
Their two faces turned toward him, and turned again
To face each other. In a moment a glaze of tears
Began to stream down Reine's, but she made no sound,
Nor raised her hand. Gore stood and stared at them,
And said, "What is it?" "Nothing important," Hoult
      said.
"Another death in the family." Reine flung her head back,

43

Except the lower jaw, which remained in place, opening
    her mouth
To a long screaming O; but only white silence
Came out of it; and Hoult said, "You gave him to me
Last night, you know." She then drew her head forward
Onto the lower jaw, closing her mouth, and she said:
"This one too?" "You'd better not speak of it,"
Hoult answered. She went to the west window and leaned
So heavily that her hand went through the pane
And the glass was heard splattering; a wind came in, with
    the odor
Of the far fire; but neither Reine nor the others
Knew that she'd gashed her hand. Gore said, "Watch
    out!" and said,
"What's the matter with her?" Reine without turning
    said, "One by one.
You are next, Father, and then the old wilderness
Will flow over this place." She flung her hands to her face,
And wept: "Oh, David. David. David." Gore shook him-
    self
As if he had gone through cobwebs, the blind gray rags
Clung on his face: "Does she mean young Larson?" Hoult
    answered wearily,
"Your guess is as good as mine," and, sighing, sat down
In the big chair. Reine said, "I betrayed him to you. I
    loved him, I loved him, I'm not ashamed.
And now he is lying up there shot in the back, and the
    blind sun
Withers his dear blue eyes. I wish I had died for you,
Dear love, dear love." She turned and said, "I'll go and
    find him,"

And she was red from her hair down to her feet, the wound
      in her hand had so spread its leakage
While she was weeping. Gore made a barking noise in his
      throat and said,
"What have you done to yourself?" She answered, "Yes,
      we made love, David and I, what harm did it do?
And Hoult killed him." Gore said, "What is it, your
      hand?" seeing the rich drops
Raining from it. "We've got to tie up your hand. Here,
      Reine. Here, Reine." Hoult leaped up and shouted,
"Keep your hands off her!" She was quiet when she heard
      his voice, and they found a handkerchief.
She let them bind up the little gash; nothing vital;
Her weeping gesture had painted her over with it. Gore
      said, "All right.
Sing your song. Go ahead." She was silent; he said,
"Make your confession." She was silent. Hoult said,
      "Dreams, old man, female dreams. You've no idea
What fancies walk in a woman's mind when she finds
      herself
Drying out of time and chance. This old faded wax flower
      have a lover?
You're very simple."

                  Reine rose up from the chair in
      which they had placed her,
And went to the long mirror at the butt of the room, and
      had even lifted her hands
To arrange her hair: she saw her starved face all blub-
      bered over
With tears and blood, the gaudy blue of her eyes
Gleaming through the red streakage; she stared and si-
      lently laughed and said,

"Ah? Poor old Europe." Hoult said, "Don't wash, my
    dear; the bombers of the next flight will be over
    you
Before you have time. Doesn't she look like a bride, old
    man?
Destruction's bride. Curious," he said, "the power-mad
Vanity of three or four politicians—who cares? You
    guessed it, Mother.
We were riding through the tall bushes in the early twi-
    light and some impulsive
Hunter took him for deer." She covered her face with her
    hands and made no sound. Gore said, "What?
    Who?
What are you talking about?" "Her blond boy," he said,
    "her little Nordic.—What is that noise?
Old man: don't you smell smoke?"

                Gore opened the eastward door and saw clouds
Driving up the wild slope in the copper light, he heard a
    distant roaring that was not the sea,
Fool not to have felt the northwest wind rise with the sun,
Caught in their evil mysteries: he sprang to the saddle
    of the horse Hoult had ridden;
He had cattle in the canyon; and swinging out from the
    house he saw the red curtain and rage of flame
Cram the gorge sea-throat. He thought, "If I had a son,
He'd help me now."

             Reine crept onto the porch behind
    Hoult, and she found him kneeling
With his rifle on the rail; he said, "Don't look. The fire
    will drive up the deer and I'll slaughter them.
This is the height of luxury. This is the way to go hunt-
    ing and stay at home." She smelled the fever-smell

46

Of his excitement and active death, mixed and more
    dreadful
With the breath of the fire, and she saw Gore
Riding the fence-trail across the canyon-head to reach
    the gate; smoke drove up the trough; terrified
    cattle
Lowed in the brush.
                    The rifle slightly shifted, stood still
    and fired; the distant rider—
His elbows flapped out like wings; he was seen to lean
    forward, his face to the crest of the running horse.
Tall bushes hid them, they reappeared, Gore had lost the
    saddle,
He had a grip on the mane and his body dragged; the
    horse reared and pivoted
And came back empty, bucking against the flap of the
    stirrups. Hoult said, "Pretty good, ah? That's
    pickin' 'em.
Three hundred yards: right in the string of the back.
Right in the loins."
                    Reine felt her mouth open
And her ribs lifting without will or intention,
As if her lungs were sucking in all the fire-smitten
Air of the planet; which then her throat moulded
Into one long monotonous and ceremonial scream. Hoult
    waited until she finished, and said,
"By God, he's tough. Observe him," for Gore was drag-
    ging himself, head up, his hands
Hauling his body, along an open space of the trail; his
    head and shoulders
Passing behind the brush-fringe, they saw the helpless
    feet inch by inch drag in the dust

47

Slowly from sight. Hoult said, "Poor old worm, the race
      is fixed.
You cannot win it. I don't hate him at all, it's justice.
I wish that every man who approved this war,
In which we had no right, reason nor justice,
Were crawling there in the fire's way with his back broken,
      and all the war-dead with all their women
Were here to watch. Look: it is God's work: I believe in
      God: he sent the fire,
He lined the sights."
                  The van of the fire now raged in
      the gorge below them; the grandeur
Eclipsed the terror; flapping sheets of clear flame flew
      from the tree-tops to farther trees or into the air
Like monstrous birds above the red hell of the under-forest;
      torrents of smoke poured up the gorge,
The fire roared like a torrent, the air was full of white
      ashes driving through dark red sunlight
In the whirls of hot wind, and now two deer were seen
Leaping out of the brush in long graceful arcs, like
      porpoises
From a green sea. Reine saw a redtail hawk
Dive from the high air into the canyon, gone mad appar-
      ently, and halfway down
Its flight-feathers caught fire; it fell like a stone,
Flame into flame. The brush at the canyon-head
Began to roar; the red backs of the cattle
Plowed to the fence and huddled and fell and were over-
      run. Gore was seen again,
Crawling on the other side, twisting his head back
To look at the leaping flames, and they covered him. Hoult
      cried, "Oh, look! It's beautiful.

48

All my strength has come back to me; I am gay as a
      bridegroom.
Come into the house." He gripped her wrist, and his hand
Hot as the fire: which all around the house had been
      checked
By trampled earth, bare rock, and the water-tank leak-
      age; but the tall calla lilies
Cooked in its heat; and the hay-barn above the house
Flowered, a high standing flame; red glared the windows
In the house darkness. Hoult said, "Come little rose, little
      white rose
Among the red ones: there are giants in these days, are
      you afraid? My corpse is huge.
It covers the western world and sprawls over Asia, people
      will hold their noses in high Mongolia
And choke in London. Come, darling. Come, little one."
      The rapid fever
Of his nerves and flesh decomposing had reached a peak
And felt its imminent fall. "Oh, quickly, quickly,
Before I am brained—brr—drained I mean—" And he
      said coldly, "I am burning up. Oh, oh, look down
      there! That's hell,
And we are in it. The boiler of life and death: you can
      see faces: there's Tojo, there's Roosevelt.
There's Captain Blasted they shot in the back.
And my old father Bull Gore, bellowing.
And your dirty little dirty doggie Davy Larson, that
      stinky spaniel, he's dead: look at him!
Like overboiled meat-bits,
Hide, hair and bones, like a pot of boiled squirrels,
All wriggling mixed. No distinction, no difference, no
      rank, no relation, no end, nothing but infamy.

49

I do not believe that any human being is rank enough
To deserve boiling." He was silent and then cried out:
        "Cover me, comfort me,
Cover me with your bed-clothes as when a child
And I was frightened. Oh, why did you ever cast me out
        of you
Into this butcher's dream?"

                        The rest is nothing
But a woman mourning a three weeks' corpse.
She was found by some Negro soldiers sent from Fort Ord
To fight the fire; they went up to the house
To fill their canteens with water, and they heard a noise
Like the howling of a small dog. They whistled to it
Through the open door: it answered and said, "Go away.
Let us alone, alone," and howled again. They stood in the
        heavy burnt-copper smoke-light
On ground bone-white with the fine snow of leaf-ashes,
And rolled their eyes at each other, big black bewildered
        conscripts from Georgia
And Alabama: their officer came and they went doubtfully
Into the house; and the hard reek of death
Led them upstairs. Reine from a thousand-year-old face
Under young hair yammered at them and said,
"Don't take my boy: he's all. He was never wicked,
He was abused." But what lay on the bed
Was only bones and corruption of what had died
On the far island; and Reine, seeing the black flesh of the
        men
And their broad-swollen lips: "Oh, you poor people,
Did the fire scorch you? Oh, oh—are you soldiers?
When they send you to fight in the third war, don't do it.

Stay at home, love each other, you must love everyone,
And apples will hang in every sycamore tree—
No matter what they have done. Even my boy
Was deceived for a time. Hush, hush, don't wake him.
His awful fever fell asleep in my arms.
You needn't roll those big eyes: nothing is wrong here,
       black men,
But kind and clean: kind, kind: we must be kind.
He melted into horror, his brain ran out
Through his nostrils: how could someone long dead
Be alive from there down?" She whined and giggled in
       her throat and said, "Oh—soldiers—
Are you dead too? That makes you black? Hm, hm, hm,
       boys—"
She made a simpering smile—"I'm not afraid of you,
Come one and all. I will lie down in the soldiers' grave-
       yard,
One, two, three, thousands, all the endless night,
War after war." And she said slyly, "Listen, soldiers,
I'll tell you something—those that cause wars are damned
As those that suffer them. See: down there, down there:
       boiling. Now I will dress myself.
I'll make some coffee for you: I didn't do so
For my own son. Please go outside the door
While I get dressed." But when they left her alone—
For she was naked before the men, with sharp white
       breasts
In the pool of brown light, and it seemed wise
To let her clothe herself if she would—they heard her
Laughing, and then a rifle-shot. She'd kissed the steel
       mouth
And fired the last of four cartridges.

THE INHUMANIST

AN old man with a double-bit axe
    Is caretaker at the Gore place. The cattle,
       except a few wild horns, died in that
       fire; the horses
Graze high up the dark hill; nobody ever comes to the
       infamous house; the pain, the hate and the love
Have left no ghost. Old men and gray hawks need solitude,
Here it is deep and wide.

1

           "Winter and summer," the old
      man says, "rain and the drought;
Peace creeps out of war, war out of peace; the stars rise
      and they set; the clouds go north
And again they go south.—Why does God hunt in circles?
      Has he lost something? Is it possible—himself?
In the darkness between the stars did he lose himself and
      become godless, and seeks—himself?"

2

"Does God exist?—No doubt of that," the old man says.
    "The cells of my old camel of a body,
Because they feel each other and are fitted together—
    through nerves and blood feel each other—all the
    little animals
Are the one man: there is not an atom in all the universes
But feels every other atom; gravitation, electromagne-
    tism, light, heat, and the other
Flamings, the nerves in the night's black flesh, flow them
    together; the stars, the winds and the people: one
    energy,
One existence, one music, one organism, one life, one God:
    star-fire and rock-strength, the sea's cold flow
And man's dark soul."

3

        "Not a tribal nor an anthropoid God.
Not a ridiculous projection of human fears, needs, dreams,
    justice and love-lust."

4

"A conscious God?—The question has no importance. But
    I am conscious: where else
Did this consciousness come from? Nobody that I know
    of ever poured grain from an empty sack.
And who, I would say, but God, and a conscious one,
Ended the chief war-makers with their war, so humor-
    ously, such accurate timing, and such

Appropriate ends? The man of vanity in vanity,
Having his portrait painted; the man of violence at vio-
      lence most dire high tide, in the fire and frenzy
Of Berlin falling."

5

           "And nothing," he thought,
"Is not alive." He had been down to the sea and hooked
      a rock-cod and was riding home: the high still
      rocks
Stood in the canyon sea-mouth alert and patient, waiting
      a sign perhaps; the heavy dark stooping hills
Shouldered the cloud, bearing their woods and streams
      and great loads of time: "I see that all things have
      souls.
But only God's is immortal. The hills dissolve and are
      liquidated; the stars shine themselves dark."

6

Cutting oak fence-posts, he stopped to whet his axe edges.
He considered the double-bladed axe: "In Crete it was a
god, and they named the labyrinth for it. That's long
before the Greeks came; the lofty Greeks were still bush-
men. It was a symbol of generation: the two lobes and the
stiff helve: so was the Cross before they christened it. But
this one can clip heads too. Grimly, grimly. A blade for
the flesh, a blade for the spirit: and truth from lies."

A sheet of newspaper
Blown from the road, the old man caught it and read at
　　arm's length, and said, "No wilderness
But this babbler comes in.—What, will they have a long
　　dusty trial
And hang the men, Goering and all his paladins: why?
　　Why?
For losing the war.
That is a fact, and Julius Caesar or Jenghiz Khan
Could be honest about it; not our gray hypocrites.
What judges, what prosecutors, what a panel!
Down, you apes, down. Down on your knee-caps, you talk-
　　ing villains, take off your eye-glasses
And beat your foreheads against the rubble ground and
　　beseech God
Forgive America, the brutal meddler and senseless de-
　　stroyer; forgive the old seamed and stinking blood-
　　guilt of England;
Forgive the deliberate torture of millions, the obscene
　　slave-camps, the endless treacheries, the cold dirty-
　　clawed cruelty
Of the rulers of Russia.—By God," he laughed, "winners
　　and losers too, what hellhounds.
What a nest this earth is." He groaned and said heavily,
"If it were mine to elect an animal to rule the earth
I'd choose tiger or cobra but nothing cruel, or skunk,
But nothing foul."

8

"What does God want?"

The old man was leaning on the dusk edge of dawn, and
the beauty of things

Smote him like a fierce wind: the heads of the mountains,
the morning star over them, the gray clearness,
the hawk-swoop

Fall of the hundred-folded ridges, night in their throats,
the deep-coiled night dying

On the dark sea—and all this hushed magnificence vio-
lently rushing eastward to meet the sunrise: "How
earnest he is.

How naïvely in earnest; nothing reserved; heavy with
destiny. Earnest as the grave eyes of a child

That doubts his mother."

"I see he despises happiness;
and as for goodness, he says, What is it? and of
evil, What is it?

And of love and hate, They are equal; they are two spurs,

For the horse has two flanks.—What does God want? I
see here what he wants: he wants what man's

Feeling for beauty wants—if it were fierce as hunger or
hate and deep as the grave."

"The beauty of things—

Is in the beholder's brain—the human mind's translation
of their transhuman

Intrinsic value. It is their color in our eyes: as we say
blood is red and blood is the life:

It is the life. Which is *like* beauty. It is *like* nobility. It
has no name—and that's lucky, for names

56

Foul in the mouthing. The human race is bound to defile,
    I've often noticed it,
Whatever they can reach or name, they'd shit on the
    morning star
If they could reach."

                    9
            "Or as mathematics, a human invention
That parallels but never touches reality, gives the astron-
    omer
Metaphors through which he may comprehend
The powers and the flow of things: so the human sense
Of beauty is our metaphor of their excellence, their divine
    nature:—like dust in a whirlwind, making
The wild wind visible."

                    10
            The heads of the high redwoods
    down the deep canyon
Rippled, instantly earthquake shook the granite-boned
    ridge like a rat
In a dog's teeth; the house danced and bobbled, lightning
    flashed from the ground, the deep earth roared,
    yellow dust
Was seen rising in divers places and rock-slides
Roared in the gorges; then all things were stilled again
    and the earth stood quiet. The old man coughed
    and said,
"Is that all? You have forgotten how to be angry: look
    again, old woman. They were not half so disgusting
The time you split your tea-kettle at Krakatoa."

11

"How quiet they are, the dead; humble and quiet; how
     careless; how quiet they are!
The most amazing and painful things
Have happened to them, they have no answer. They go
     aside and lie down in silence and shrink to nothing."
The old man had gone upstairs in the house to trace a
     roof-leak
That stained the planks; he moved in the stale air and
     still rooms, among the little personal possessions
With dust on them. A man and his wife and their son had
     lived here; "Now I could take an axe and split all
To splinters; they would not lift one word nor one finger."

                              "Time will come, no doubt,
When the sun too shall die; the planets will freeze, and
     the air on them; frozen gases, white flakes of air
Will be the dust: which no wind ever will stir: this very
     dust in dim starlight glistening
Is dead wind, the white corpse of wind.
Also the galaxy will die; the glitter of the Milky Way,
     our universe, all the stars that have names are
     dead.
Vast is the night. How you have grown, dear night, walk-
     ing your empty halls, how tall!"

12

A skeleton with hair and teeth, a black hound-bitch
Crawled from a bush and grovelled at the old man's feet:
     he was in the dooryard, admiring

The vast red ostentation of a December sundown, and
  when he looked, the dog's eyes
Were green with famine. He said, "You have been be-
  trayed by someone? But hungry freedom
Is better than a bad master." She moaned in her throat;
  he went in and fetched food, but the first bite,
The long teeth pierced his hand, blood ran on the
  knuckles: then he laughed and said,
"What? Are you human?" She erected all the hair on her
  back, snarling, and sprang; and was kicked down
And stood crying, far off. "Neither," he said, "am I: not
  entirely,"—sopping the bread
In his own blood for savor, and he tossed it to her.

                                              In the
          morning she was at the door; he fed her and said,
"Go your ways," but she would not. He said, "You are
  fed and free: go your ways," and flung stones at
  her, but she
Crawling returned. He said, "Must you have security
  also? Stay, slave."

13

Trespassers

From time to time crossed the place, then the dog yelled
  at them
And the man drove them off. One stayed to argue. "The
  land," he said, "belongs to the people; we make
  its value.
I am one of the people." The old man listened to his axe
  and said, "You are the people.
You are Caligula's dream: only one neck. Listen, fellow:

This land is clean, it is not public. Surely you've noticed
        that whatever is public, land, thoughts or women,
Is dull, dirty and debauched. And it is not *my* land: I have
        nothing
But an axe and a dog: I am the people-stopper. I tell you
        that exclusion and privilege
Are the last bleeding clawhold of the eagle, honor." Then
        the man thought, "He is mad and he has an axe:
I will not vex him."

14

                    But a day of black wind and rain
Another transgressor came; he was trembling with cold
        and blue with terror: "Let me pass, I am hunted.
I am going to the hills to hide, I know a cave.
I killed my wife and her lover." "Two," the old man said,
        "out of two thousand million. Do you see those
        horns
Coming over the hill? That's the third world-war. It is
        not worth fearing and not worth welcoming,
Futile as you, it will not kill one in ten."
                    But after the man had passed he thought:
"Ah, can I never swallow that lump the people? I am old
        and deaf, but the huge music might miss
Their gnashing treble.—But two thousand million!"

15

                    In the morning soft, white and staring snow
Lay on the ridges above the wet black slopes; the distant
        mountain-summits glittered like wolves' teeth

In the gray sky. The old man rejoiced and said, "In this
      pure world . . . In this pure world . . . O axe,
You are not needed." The axe twitched and giggled in his
      hand as if it were saying, "You pure old innocence:
Because your hair has gone white, holy is whiteness."
      "No," he answered, "my eyes are snail-eyes, they
      are outside of me.
Man is no measure of anything. Truly it is yours to hack,
      snow's to be white, mine to admire;
Each cat mind her own kitten, that is our morals. But
      wait till the moon comes up the snow-tops
And you'll sing Holy."

16
                    The old man heard
An angry screaming in heaven and squinted upward,
      where two black stars
Hunted each other in the high blue; they struck and
      passed,
Wheeled and attacked again; they had great hate of each
      other; they locked and fell downward and came
      apart,
And spiralled upward, hacking with beaks and hooks and
      the heavy wings: they were two eagles:
He watched them drift overhead, fighting, to the east,
And pass from view. Then the old man said, "Today I
      shall meet someone I know." He considered and
      said:
"How do I know that? Because any omen or senseless
      miracle, any strange cry or sight
Stretches the mind: we feel the future through the
      strained fabric."

61

17

In the evening when he came home,
There was a little fire in the dooryard and a tall girl
Stood up beside it. She had dark hair, doe eyes, and was
    minding a pot
That seethed on three stones over the coal-bed. The old
    man stood silent, gazing at her; his dog at his knee
Made a low throat of wrath. The girl answered and said,
    "Come.
Supper is ready." "Yea," he said, "for whom?" He saw
    the evening planet
Beside her shoulder in the deep-throated rose of the sea,
    and said more gently:
"Eat if you are hungry, but you cannot stay here. I am
    not stone yet." She answered, "Don't you
Remember me? I do you." "No," he said, "a gipsy?" "I
    am the Spanish woman's little girl.
You called me Gaviota, Father." He sighed and answered:
"My eagles did not tell me that. I thought I could live
    alone and enjoy old age. First a dog: now a
    daughter:
And tomorrow a canary!" He looked attentively and said:
    "Your eyes, Sea-gull, have lamps in 'em. It's not
    for love
Of your father's old bones." ˙

18

For no apparent reason an army bombing-plane
Pitched from the sky and exploded on the rock-ridge
Below the peak. The old man at that time was riding not
    far away; he followed the smoke-tree

To its hot yellow root. A spirit in the fire sang,
"O Kittyhawk." The old man mocked it and said,
"O Hiroshima." It sang, "O San Francisco, Seattle, New
       York." He answered, "O stony goat-pastures.
But not tomorrow nor o' Monday. But," he said, dis-
       mounting,
And kneeling on the sharp rock his old knotted shin-bones,
       "O holy fire, the cruel, the kind, the coarse feeder,
O cleansing fire."

19

               That blown-over tower of smoke, a
       swollen black leech clinging
By its hot yellow teeth to the mountain's neck, was seen
       far off
Along the shores and ridges and by ships at sea. A woman
       named Dana Enfield saw it, and rode
With her brother Bill Stewart to see the crashed plane;
       they took the bushed-over shortcut, not for years
       used,
Up Llagas Ridge; and where it clears on the cliffhead
       they saw the white mane of a tied horse
In the green gorge below. Stewart looked, grinned and
       rode on; Dana checked and said:
"Is there any other palomino in these mountains?
What is he doing down there?" "Oh, after some cow,"
       he said, "—or heifer." He saw her face
Grown sharp and sallow: she had a fox-pointed chin, pale
       lips, yellow-dusk hair
And yellow eyes: she said, "I have never spied on him
       nor listened to you

63

When you snickered and hinted. Will you go down and
    see?" "Yea?" he said.
"To hell with that." She answered, "What a coward you
    are when you are sober," wheeling her horse
On the precipice brink so blindly that stones fell: a bitter
    woman of forty, seeing in her mind
A long white child like a peeled willow-fork: it was the
    panting mouth
That made her sick: but in the dark of her mind more
    dreadful presences, this war and this peace,
A monster leading a monster to the monster's house, pro-
    ceed.

20

            The old man leaned on his axe and watched
Certain brown canvas bundles, the bodies of six young
    men lashed on three horses,
Come down the bend of the mountain to the airforce truck
Parked at the drivehead. It is curious how things repeat
    themselves, but always changed: it was thus Bull
    Gore's
And David Larson's were borne down the burnt moun-
    tain; their escort soldiers were Negro and these
    were white;
That was in time of war, this of so-called peace: it made
    no difference;
The horses went foot by foot, the men who rode them
    were dead.
                 The old man's daughter
Led the first horse; when she came down he called to her
    and said:

64

"Listen, Sea-gull: there was a yellow-eyed woman here
        asking for you. The truth is too precious
To be spent on such people: so I told her
That you'd gone back to town. I am not sure whose creek
        you are fishing in, little one:
Look out for snags."

21

                        Like the steep necks of a herd of horses
Lined on a river margin, athirst in summer, the mountain-
        ridges
Pitch to the sea, the lean granite-boned heads
Plunge nostril-under: on the rock shore between two great
        heads
Stands the Stewart ranch-house in its canyon-mouth,
Tall, cube-shaped and unadorned, painted dull yellow,
And the creek runs below. It is here that yellow-eyed
        woman lives,
With her two brothers and her new husband,
And her daughter Vere Harnish.
                        Vere came up from the creek
Carrying a wet towel, her light-brown hair
Hung lank and wet; a narrow-hipped girl of sixteen or
        so, broad-faced, and thick
Eyelids that made the eyes reticent slits: she drew back-
        ward into the gorge-bank bushes,
Hearing leather creak, wishing not to be seen, and
        watched a horseman
Go by; it was Clive Enfield, her mother's husband, riding
        his beautiful palomino,

A hawk-faced young man with a silvered bridle and a red
neck-cloth.
His quick eyes could not miss her; he waved and passed
and went up the canyon. Presently she heard the
night-herons,
That roost all day in the canyon-throat wood, indignantly
shouting. They hate every passer-by
Under their private forest; two or three flew up
Over the tree-tops, great birds with soft owly wings,
Wheeling and cawing.

                    Vere Harnish went on,
And met her mother by the side of the house, who said
flat-voiced,
"Which way did he go?" "Who?" she answered sullenly.
        "Clive," she answered. "Did he go by the road
Or up the canyon?" "Your husband," she answered, "that
great lover, that slicked-up and perfumed tramp.
Mother,
How you degrade yourself!" Who blazed at her
With her clear yellow eyes and said flat-voiced, "Did he
go up the canyon? I thought I heard
The herons squawk." "You heard a crow or a gull. I liked
you once, Mother, I even respected you.
Now I will go and wash again." "Who," she answered,
"Made you my judge? Did I neglect you when you were
little? Did I neglect your father when he lay dying
Month after month?" "And in six months another man.
        I wish you had. You are horrible, Mother,
All twittering with love and jealousy . . . Ah, ah, ah,"
        she moaned, "Ah,
Please yourself."

66

22

A cold night of no moon and great
stars, crystals in granite, and little foxes down the
dark mountain
Singing from ridge to ridge, the distant ocean sighing in
her sleep, the old man looked up
At a black eyelet in the white of the Milky Way, and he
thought with wonder: "There—or thereabout—
Cloaked in thick darkness in his power's dust-cloud,
There is the hub and heavy nucleus, the ringmaster
Of all this million-shining whirlwind of dancers, the stars
of this end of heaven. It is strange, truly,
That great and small, the atoms of a grain of sand and
the suns with planets, and all the galactic universes
Are organized on one pattern, the eternal roundabout, the
heavy nucleus and whirling electrons, the leashed
And panting runners going nowhere; frustrated flight,
unrelieved strain, endless return—all—all—
The eternal fire-wheel."
While he considered the matter,
staring upward, and the night's noises
Hushed, there came down from heaven a great virile cry,
a voice hoarser than thunder, heavily reverberated
Among the star-whorls and cliffs of darkness: "I am
caught. I am in the net." And then, intolerably
patient:
"I see my doom."
The old man trembled and laughed,
gaping upward: "My God: have they got Oedipus
Or Lear up there? Was it a cry of nature? Is it possible
that man's passion is only a reflex of

Much greater torment; and what was shouted among the
    stars comes dwindling and tottering down
Into human jaws and a king's bursting heart—or a
    lynched black's:—very likely: hates, loves and
    world-wars—
Hypnotized players: look at their vacant eyes:
Of obscure tragedies that being uncomprehended echoes
    of misheard fragments are nonsense.
But the great voice was in earnest."

23

The rain paused about dawn, the southeast wind raged
    like an axe, there was no sleep
In the tumult of storm and the house trembling. Vere
    Harnish dressed and went down, she stood and
    stared
From a west window at the mud-yellow sky streaked with
    flying cloud, and black under foam-sheets
The beaten sea; she heard the south window hiss in the
    pelting
Of twigs and gravel, she thought it might burst presently.
Her mother, Dana Enfield, came in half-dressed;
They had no eyes for each other and sat stiffly apart,
    staring
At the west window: branches of trees and formless rags
    of foam fled
Down the dark light, and streaks of yellow floodwater now
    became visible below the foam-drift
On the sea's beaten face: but all this rage of the air,
No air to breathe.
                At that moment an undreamed-of thing

like a flying cowhide
Came dark on the south window and smashed it; glass-
fragments rained, chairs fell, Dana Enfield
Fled from the room; Vere sat frozen and saw a huge bird
Snared in its broken wing wrestling against the wall-foot;
a pelican, the nine-foot-spread bird
With the great beak; it had been cropped from a sea-rock,
and the iron draught
On the cliffhead had caught it. Birds have their fates like
men, and this one
Destined from the egg to die in a human house—as the
last Czar in a cellar, or Goering the luxurious
On a cast-iron jail-cot—had met its appointment. Vere
stood up coldly in the whirlwind, she also
Under compulsion, she felt through two drawers and
found a knife.
Sholto Stewart
Came into the room up the insane wind,
And Vere was on her knees in the room wreckage, mechani-
cally pumping the penknife blade
Through the bird's bloody breast. Her mouth hung open
like a dead clam-shell, she had no look of anything
But dull duty well done. She said, "It smells like fish-
blood, it nearly mothers me."

24

A gray-haired walker with an erect backbone and benevo-
lent spectacles
Paced up the hill to the Gore place; the old axeman
watched him and went to meet him: "What do *you*
want?" He answered:

69

"Advice, advice. I am a man much troubled about the
future. I believed we were building peace,
And suddenly fantastic expressions of death and horror
pop up like jumping-jacks
On all horizons. Our minds and our words go wrong, the
peace has gone wrong, these years are deadly:
What can we do?" "*Me* you ask?" "Because they say you
have a harsh wisdom, unperfumed, untuned, un-
taught,
Like Heraclitus's Sibyl." "Whose voice," the old man
answered, "reaches over ten thousand years
Because of the God." "Well," he said, "more or less."
"Who," the old man answered, "was Heraclitus? I
have some wisdom—
In the head of my axe." "I am more humble than you,"
he answered,
"I am willing to be taught, and I am willing to teach, and
the world wants wisdom. The axe
Is in its root." The old man sighed and smiled: "I have
noticed that." "What can we do," he answered,
"To save the world? What has gone wrong with our peace?
Why do we grin at the Russians and they at us?
All hangs on that." The old man counted his fingers:
"France, England, Germany. Japan. You and the Rus-
sians.
There were six powers in the world, and peace was pos-
sible. You could have forced it and kept it, even
when France fell,
But you preferred victory. Thence your two giants, alone
in the rubble world, watching each other
For the weak moment." He groaned and said, "You are

70

wrong. You are twice wrong. Why cannot two
friends in victory,
Two friends be friends?" "Two bulls in one herd?" he an-
swered. "But these," he said, "are people. We have
minds." The old man
Laughed, and the other patiently: "Which side is evil
then?
We or the others?" "Two stallions," the old man answered,
"in a run of mares: which side is evil?" "Well," he
said, "the Aggressor."
"I see you are superstitious," he answered, "you believe in
words. But words
Are like women: they are made to lie with." "I under-
stand at least," he answered, "that you utterly
despair.
If nations have no morality, and words no meaning, and
women
No other purpose." "Look down there," the old man an-
swered, "on the green ridge, the second ridge.
Do you see the ivory-colored horse and the horseman—
and the tall girl
Running to meet him?" "What?" he said. "Yes, I see."
"Look," the old man said, "look how she leans
Her breast on the rider's thigh and his arm embraces her.
Pretty, ah? It's even beautiful. Her name is Sea-
gull.
She opens her little beak, she is gulping for love. She has
no mind but an instinct. She will drop twins,
The race will live, though civilization burns like a straw-
stack." "Does that please you?" He twitched his
shoulder, saying, "Me?
Had *I* a choice?

71

I think the whole human race ought to be scrapped and is
            on the way to it; ground like fish-meal for soil-
            food.
What does the vast and rushing drama of the universe,
            seas, rocks, condor-winged storms, ice-fiery gal-
            axies,
The flaming and whirling universe like a handful of gems
            falling down a dark well,
Want clowns for? Hah?"

25

                The old iron crowbar driven into the mountain
To mark a corner of the Gore place had been forced and
            disrooted: whether by some intruder, or the sleepy
            rock
Moved underground, or a wild boar had moved it, rooting
            by moonlight. The old man hammered it home
            again,
And heaped a cairn of stones above it to guard it. There
            were fine stones on that ridge: the old man found
            himself
Taking an artist pleasure in his little pyramid, and said
            to himself:
"To whom this monument: Jesus or Caesar or Mother
            Eve?
No," he said, "to Copernicus: Nicky Kupernick: who first
            pushed man
Out of his insane self-importance and the world's navel,
            and taught him his place."

                        "And the next one to Darwin."

26

Sholto Stewart was repairing the window
The bird had broken; he had putty and a pane of glass,
And was taking down the planks he had nailed for shelter
While the storm raged. His sister Dana Enfield came
     suddenly
Around the corner of the house; her face looked haggard
     green in the sea-shine, her drab-yellow
Hair was uncombed and her yellow eyes turbid: "He's
     gone again
Up the mountain to meet her. Sholto, Sholto," she caught
     his arm,
"Get me rid of that hill-crawler!" "Yea?" he said, "I told
     you
Before you married him." "I mean," she said, "the bitch.
     Clive loves me but he is soft.
It is the bitch." He answered, "A cunning morsel, mud,
     rags and all. I never liked him,
But I can see his point." "She is horrible," she answered;
     and stood and stared at the sea-glitter, her lips
     twitching
On silence: the way that lonely-hobbling old women, tur-
     bulent and undesired and remembering,
Talk to themselves. The man turned back to his work,
And drew with the claws of the hammer another nail; the
     wire shank screamed
In the wet wood. At the same moment a sea-gull mewed in
     the air. Dana breathed and said,
"Lend me your hammer, Sholto." "What?" he said, de-
     taching it
From another nailhead, and he gave it to her: she instantly

73

Swung it against the pane of glass at the wall-foot; the
    bright sheet flashed
In jags and fragments. "Well," he said, "what a woman."
        "I couldn't help it," she answered, "the handle
Slid in my hand." "So you say, Mrs. Fury." "Oh, it's my
        fault," she answered; "I'll have to send
Clive to town for more glass. While he's gone, Sholto,
We'll have a party. I have three or four quarts
Put away for New Year's: this will be New Year's,
I hope and pray."

                Hope, as the old man said, is a great
        folly. It is often the wickedest
Hopes that prevail, as gardens liefer bear weeds than
        fruit, but good or evil, they are weighted
With equal fear. It is far better, therefore, the old man
        said, not to complicate
Action with expectation, but go on by instinct. What
        comes will come.
The great bear and the sabre-tooth tiger, the powerful
        ones perish; an absurd ape drops from a tree
And for a time rules the earth.

27

                Sea-gull: because a horse's hide is the color
Of ancient ivory, and his mane and his tail white as a wave
        and a torrent: it does not prove
That his rider is with him. Be careful, Sea-gull.

                But she, when she looked down the mountain
And saw the palomino on the green ridge in the winter
        sun-gleam tethered and beautiful,
Had no distrust; she ran on the side-hills and hastened

In the leaf-green barranca, she heard a trampling
In the bushes behind her: "Oh, Clive, where are you?" but
      it was Sholto Stewart
Grinning on a bay horse, whirling his rope, and the noose
      flew,
But she escaped it. She fled and two men on foot pushed
      through the leaves; one was young and dark-
      skinned,
A Spanish boy: she turned to him and smelled whiskey
      and said, "Que hay, amigo?" He in English
Giggled, "It is a peekneek. You are invite," and caught
      her by the slim wrist. She strove against him,
But the older man, heavy and red, with bloodshot blue
      eyes,
Lurched alongside her, Sholto rode hard behind, they ran
      her down to a clearance
Where two horses were tied and that yellow-eyed woman,
      Dana Enfield, came under a tan-oak tree
Saying, "Here you are. A long time I've tried to find you.
      Until my husband lent me his horse:
He said you'd come." "No," she said. "Oh, but he did,"
      she answered. "Do you think he cares for you?
      You were his plaything,
His dirty, dirty toy and he laughs at you. How could I
      know about you
Unless he told me?" The girl shook her head silently,
      writhing her arm in the hands that held it, beauti-
      ful
In the upward-beating soft golden sea-light, for the sun
      was clouded. A heavy wedge of dark hair fell for-
      ward

On her thin face; her worn shirt, torn at the throat, ex-
posed
The thrust of the fine shoulder; and Sholto Stewart, now
dismounted,
Stared at her, licking his hard thin lips, and the others
held her. But Dana saw nothing beautiful in her,
But answered hoarsely: "He did though: he gave you to
me. Men like to amuse themselves with little dirty
ones,
Rags, bones and smell, but when it's in earnest, when it
comes to the pinch, they choose a clean woman,
A person of some honor and importance. All right: he
chose. He gave you to me. I'll tell you
What we are going to do." Her pale yellow eyes
Blazed hard and little, suddenly the reined-in wrath over-
came her
And she shook like a flame: "You cast-off rag-doll. You
dirt-queen." Her hand flashed and she struck
The thin young face: "You soiled hill-crawler." Bill Stew-
art said heavily,
"Easy, Sis, take it easy." Then Sea-gull, with tears in the
under-lids
Of her long eyes, and on her lip a small fleck of blood:
"You needn't waste anger on me. Oh, why?
I never harmed you, I never saw you before, I never spoke
of you. I was happy to take the bits
Under your table." Suddenly the Spanish boy laughed
like a fool; Dana Enfield glanced at him
And said to Sea-gull: "You're going to be whipped until
you roar. Bring the rope, Sholto.
You're going to go away and never come back. Take your
sore back

76

Out of these hills." Bill Stewart said heavily,
"You said that you would talk to her. To hell with whip-
ping.
Whipping's for horses." "Until she's raw," she answered,
"until she falls,
And then awhile." The Spanish boy Louie Lopez said
solemnly,
"You are dronk, Mrs. Enfiel'?" But Sholto, his meagre
face twitching one side, from the right eye
To the corner of the mouth, came with his rope and stood
swaying and said, "This is it, Frowline." Bill
Stewart
Stood back from her; Lopez stood forward, saying, "You
are dronk. You will not do it." Sholto answered,
"Off," and his free hand suddenly striking forward took
the girl's shirt, the neckband behind the shoulder,
And tore it from her; she cried bitterly three times:
"Clive, help! Clive, help!" Dana answered, "He hears you.
He will not help you. Tie her up to the tree, Sholto: I wish
the quirt
Were boiled in salt." The Spanish boy wildly laughed
again,
Staring at the bared breasts: "I tell you. We take her
Into the bushes. Ah? Ah?" He was all at once as pale as
his corpse would be; yellow gray. Sholto
Handling the rope said, "Hold out your hands, Frow-
line." Then Sea-gull turned and began to run,
but Lopez
Tripped her first step and fell with her. She fought
against him
On the ground in sharp silence. He tore open her blue-
jeans

77

And was dragging them down; Dana cried fiercely, "You
  half-wit.
You drunken swine," and Sholto, hooking his hands on
  the boy's throat, subtracted him
From what he sought. "Wait for your turn." He knelt by
  Sea-gull
And struck her throat with his fist. Dana gasped and said,
"When you're done with her, call me." She turned away
  a few steps, and stood
Looking down toward the sea. The sun hung in the cloud-
  bank a huge red disk, and across the water
A red causeway ran out to it; the mountainfoot shore
Was blue as dreams.

        While up the slope that bestiality—
  I mean, that humanity—
Man and no other animal—performed itself. Louie Lopez
Stood leaning forward, gazing religiously
At the girl's sprawled white legs and her gasping face;
  Bill Stewart on the other side stood like an ox,
His little blue eyes staring at nothing, his red jowls rumi-
  nant, chewing his cud
Like an old ox that the butcher has forgotten: but after
  his brother and the Spanish boy finished
He took his turn. Then Lopez felt new desire and spent it.
  Sholto said, "Get up,"
But he would not, and Sholto with the whip flicked him;
  he stood up sullenly
And drew his clothing together. Sholto's breath hissed
As he striped the girl's flank: one stripe: and Lopez
Sprang at his throat. While they fought, clumsy with
  drunkenness,

78

Sea-gull fled naked into the brush to the north
And hid herself until nightfall; she went home wearily
And lay and slept. In the morning the old man, her father,
Said, "Why were you crying, Sea-gull? What happened
　　to you?" "Oh, no," she answered.
He said, "Was he unkind to you?" "Oh, no," she answered,
Turning her face from him. "What bruised your face?"
　　"I fell in a bush of trees
From a tall rock."

28

　　　　　　　　It rained all night and coyotes gath-
　　ered, snapping and scritching
At the doors of the house; yet his black hound-bitch, the
　　old man
In common kindness had brought in-doors, never rebuked
　　them; and in the morning he said:
"Snapper, you are too happy, you are too American. You
　　need a little sleet on your hide,
And to taste hunger." She, drooping her ears and tail,
　　trotted behind him, but at noon vanished. In the
　　evening
Thunder from ridge to ridge leaped like a goat and bursts
　　of hail
Whipped the hills white. Snapper had not come home; in
　　the darkness the weather worsened; coyotes appar-
　　ently
Fought a pitched battle, and complete with screams of
　　the dying, right at the house-door. The old man
　　went out,

And all but the dark wind and sharp sleet was peace. But
at dawn he looked out and saw

What darkness hid: the torn corpse of a dog in a cirque
of bushes; gnawn, blood-smeared, the ears bitten
off

And the teeth glaring. "This is strange. It is not Snapper.
Do you know him, Sea-gull?" She, on the doorstep,

Hooded with a blanket for the shrill air: "Where did he
come from?

What happened to him?" "I think," he said, "he died for
love,

Like a fellow in a play." "Look," she answered. Far away
up the hill Snapper was seen

Coming down delicately between the black bushes in the
gray light

From the dark dawn. She sniffed the carcass daintily and
came to the house, ears lowered. The old man
answered:

"How should I know that you were singing a love-song

In the throat under your tail and with musk for music?
But the wolves heard you, and that stark hero,
wherever

He comes from, heard." She looked up and laughed doubt-
fully, as a dog does; and Sea-gull: "Oh, she is hurt.

There is blood on her jaw." "Not hers," he said, "nor a
wolf's either.

She has been a traitress, and in spring she'll drop wolf-
cubs.

The world reverts. Dogs and men tire of a slow decline."
So he said. There was in fact a more merciless

And more life-weary beauty in the vast landscape, the
dark gray light, the one dull streak of sulphur for
dawn, 80

Dark headlong slopes, the black-fanged rocks and high
  grinning snow-teeth, the long row of the snow-
  struck mountain-tops

High up in heaven. The old man looked up. "Am I also
  a renegade? I prefer God to man.

But," he said grimly, "Snapper, I have not tasted

Any cannibal feasts. It is the people-lovers and nation-
  leaders, the human-centered,

Have bloody chops." He sighed and said, "In this pale
  light

All the little tricks are played out and finished. Retreat
  is no good, treachery no good, goodness no good.

But still remains the endless inhuman beauty of things;
  even of humanity and human history

The inhuman beauty—and there is endurance, endurance,
  death's nobler cousin. Endurance."

29

Sea-gull awoke to an angry noise of grinding in the deep
  night, and lay still,

Loving her own bare body warm in the bed, how clean and
  alive it was; nor man's brutality

Nor sky's hardship had numbed it; she thought that noth-
  ing could—

But that's youth's dream—and soon, the high angry noise
  continuing,

She stood up barefoot and wrapped the blanket around
  her and went to look. She found her old father

Working the treadle grindstone behind the house, grind-
  ing an axe, leaning the steel on the stone

So that it screamed, and a wild spray of sparks

Jetted on the black air. "What are you doing to your axe,
     Father?" He would not hear her; she clutched
His hard shoulder and drove the fingernails in. "Why are
     you grinding your axe, Father,
In the deep night?" He turned a contorted face and said,
"It is not mine. Why should I ruin mine?
This is a rust-headed skull that the former people
Left in the shed." The steel screamed and she shouted,
     "Why are you grinding it?" "I hate, and I want
     to kill."
"Whom are you going to kill?" "No one," he groaned.
     "Who is worth killing? I am sick tonight, I am
     human:
There is only one animal that hates himself. Truly the
     sweating toad and poison-gorged pit-viper
Are content with their natures. I'll be a stone at the bot-
     tom of the sea, or any bush on the mountain,
But not this ghost-ridden blood-and-bone thing, civil war
     on two legs and the stars' contempt, this walking
     farce,
This ape, this—denatured ape, this—citizen—" He
     stooped over the stone, the steel screamed like a
     horse, and the spark-spray
Spouted from the high hill over land and sea. It was like
     the glittering night last October
When the earth swam through a comet's tail, and fiery
     serpents
Filled half of heaven. But in the morning Sea-gull said:
     "What was the matter with you, Father, last
     night?"
"You are mistaken," the old man answered. "Possibly you
     saw my ghost: it may have gone out of me,

82

For I slept like a rock."

He looked up and down

At the cold peaks lining the lonely sky, and that opaque
gray monster the ocean, incessantly

Gnawing his rocks. "Is it not enough? I see that the world
is very beautiful, great and—in earnest.

It bred man and surrounds him and will reabsorb him:
what more do I want?—It bred," he answered
himself,

"Louse too: noble and ignoble, the eagle and her lice.
What more I want is a little nobility in man

To match the world's." He looked again at the great land-
scape and laughed. "I am asking something.

Nevertheless—

Every tragic poet has believed it possible. And every
Savior, Buddha down to Karl Marx,

Has preferred peace. Tragedy, shall we say, is a cult of
pain, and salvation of happiness:

Choose and be sifted.

But I will be turned again to the
outer magnificence, the all but inhuman God.

I will grind no more axes."

30

The tide ran out, leaving a
forest of tumbled rocks, wet fur and brown weed,

Where late ran the tall waves. Sholto Stewart and Clive
Enfield came down from the house

To gather shellfish, and soon Enfield came back with a
sack of mussels, along the slippery

And whale's-back reef. At the angle of the cliff by the
    creek sand-beach he met Vere Harnish,
His wife's daughter, coming stiffly to meet him, her broad
    face greenish white, her hands huddled up
Against her breast. Her mouth, with the white lips drawn
    on the teeth,
Moved like a fish's mouth. Clive dropped the briny-
Dripping sack from his shoulder and said, "My God—
What is the matter?" She moved her mouth like a fish two
    or three times on silence, and moaned:
"It hurts me so. Kiss me, Clive, I am dying." She opened
    her hands at him,
And they were full of blood from the slashed wrists; noth-
    ing arterial, shallow razor-cuts
That would heal in a fortnight: and Enfield knew it: but
    he bawled for Sholto;
And heard with dull contempt his own voice
Beating between the sea and the mountain like a mournful
    bird.

31

Wildcat, coon and coyote, deer and wild pig, weasel and
    civet-cat, the stalking puma and the dainty foxes,
Traveled together, they all went the one way. On the
    other side of the rock a dense-packed river
Of humanity, all races, brown, white, black, yellow, flowed
    along the wide ridge
In the opposite direction. The old man leaned on the rock,
    watching both ways. He heard the sad animals
In their innocence hum to each other, "We are going into
    the past, into the past, we have no place

In the great age." Therefore he turned to the others and
    said,
"Where are you going?" "Into the future with the dawn
    on our faces. Come along with us." "No," he said.
They answered, "Will you go with the beasts then?"
    "Certainly not," he answered. "I would break both
    my legs
Liefer than go with beasts or men or angels *en masse*.
    What are you seeking?"
"The future, the human future." "You'll be surprised,"
    he said.
        "However," he said, "time is a ring:
    what's future?
And when again you meet the beasts on this pleasant hill,
    the fox yaps in your faces, your harps are hushed,
    future is past—
I shall be here."

32

The palomino and his rider with a led horse, a gelding
    sorrel, came up the hill-drive
Toward the ranch-house. The old man did not see them;
    he saw his daughter staring, her hands at her
    throat;
He took his axe and stood beside her and saw the two
    horses. "Well, Sea-gull. I think your wings
Lift from this rock." She made no answer; he said, "Are
    you happy?" She made no answer, her eyes
Pinned on the nearing rider. The old man said impa-
    tiently, "Instinctive female: in all this magnificence
Of sea and mountain—one man." Her lover at the head

of the drive let in the spurs; he ran the level, reined hard,

And said from the rearing saddle, "Come on, Gaviota."
    She ran to him, he leaned and kissed her and said,

"Get your stuff and we'll go." "Nothing," she said; "I had clean clothes but I lost them

The other day; they were torn all to pieces. Darling, if I had nothing at all I'd ride with you

Naked." "Yea," he said, "cold but beautiful." The old man said, "Remember, Sea-gull: if he turns bad,

Or goes to live in a city, you can come back here. Where are you going?" Clive answered him:

"We'll flip a nickel. All I know is, it's time.

I have been seduced by a chlorotic brat, and knocked my brother-in-law's

Teeth down his throat— What did they do to you, Sea-gull, the other day?" "Oh," she said, "nothing.

I think they wanted to beat me; I got away." "Besides," he said, "I am very weary

Of that yellow-eyed woman every night draining me." The old man said,

"Be warned, Sea-mew: be moderate." She in her golden haze of joy overflowing gold

Suddenly flung herself on her father and embraced him, "Good-bye, good-bye," worming her body against him,

Crushing the fine grapes of her breasts

On his old ribs. He groaned across her dark hair to Enfield, "Look here, young man:

Give her a baby soon or she'll melt the rocks"—but she had already left him, and leaped

To the saddle of the sorrel, and they went their way.
                                        The old man heard
A crying against his knee and looked down at the eyes
Of his black hound-bitch; he said, "You are wrong, Snap-
        per. It is no harm. We shall have less distraction
        now.
Death and departure are not evil things. I tell you sadly,
        every person that leaves
A place, improves it: the mourners at every funeral know
        that
In their shamed hearts: and when the sociable races of
        man and dog are done with, what a shining wonder
This world will be."

33

                        But the hound's eyes wavered from
        him, and suddenly
Grew fixed and wild; the black hair on her back stood like
        a hedge and her teeth like knives: the old man
Looked then, and saw himself, or an image of himself, tall,
        bony and repulsive to him, trough cheeks, gray
        beard-stubble,
And whitish gray eyes in sagging eye-slots: he like the
        hound flinched backward. "Did I say undistracted!
We send the living away: dummies and shadows
Pop up out of the ground. Can you talk?" "Yes," it said
        gravely. "What do you say then?" "That you are
        not honest.
If you in truth believed that man is a nuisance and life
        an evil—you'd act." "Act then," he answered.

87

"You know," it answered, "I cannot: I am a phantom."

"You are a phantom," he said, "you will be gone
In five minutes: and the human race in a million years:
        and I in twenty: we phantoms."
"But," he said, "as to action—truly the world is full of
        things the mind must know
And the hand must not do. Come, fool: be patient.
Life is not logic."

34

            Sholto's aching mouth kept him awake;
        light footsteps and candle-flicker
Went up the passage; a bedroom conversation began; he
        lay and grinned
Painfully in the dark. A crazy cluster of screams got him
        up. One door-sill was light-lined,
His sister's room, he went and pushed wide the door and
        saw the candle on the dresser, and Vere Harnish
Kneeling against the bed beside her mother's half-naked
        body, pumping a pen-knife into it,
As she had done to that storm-blown bird. There was a
        good deal of blood, and Sholto stood
In the room and howled. Then Vere stood up, saying, "I
        loved my mother, but a certain thing happened,
She had to die. I have my reasons. She was a bad influence,
I have no respect for her." She passed him unhindered,
        and heard his brother Bill Stewart panting like a
        hill-climber
In the house darkness, and passed him.

35

Rain-gray and dark the dawn, but for some reason
The old man's heart melted; he stood at gaze, his frost-
gray eyes
Warm and hollow as a cow's. He leaned on his axe and
slowly turned himself from the noble hill-tops
To the gray eye of the ocean, the gray rivers of mist in
the branching gorges, the tall black rocks
Gray-based, and the still lakes of pale silver air, and
slowly back again
To the nobility of the hill-tops. Suddenly he knelt, and
tears ran down the gullied leather
Of his old cheeks. "Dear love. You are so beautiful.
Even this side the stars and below the moon. How can you
be . . . all this . . . and me also?
Be human also? The yellow puma, the flighty mourning-
dove and flecked hawk, yes, and the rattlesnake
Are in the nature of things; they are noble and beautiful
As the rocks and the grass—not this grim ape,
Although it loves you.—Yet two or three times in my life
my walls have fallen—beyond love—no room for
love—
I have been you."
His dog Snapper
Pitied him and came and licked his loose hand. He pushed
her off:
"I have been *you*, and you stink a little."

36

A small sharp light flashed on the black-green mountain
Opposite the morning sun: the old man looked attentively
      and rode down to it, and found a stranger
With glittering concave glasses on white-lashed eyes, who
      spoke from the back of his throat: "Is here not
      free either?
I do no harm here." The old man considered him and said,
      "But plenty elsewhere: is that it?" "Ach, no," he
      answered,
"I haf escaped. Is now with me clean science or nothing;
      I serve no more." "But you did serve," he said,
"Death, while it lasted." "While it lasted?" he answered.
      "It lasts, it lasts.
That you will see." "You are not telling me news," the
      old man answered, and listened to his axe
As one listens to a watch whether it ticks, and he held it
      toward him: "Do you hear it?" The foreigner
      heard it
Humming and yelping to itself, and stepped backward
      from it: "What for a thing is that?" "A hungry
      eagle-chick,"
The old man said, "yelping to itself." The foreigner's
      glasses flashed in the sun as he shook his head:
"It is not scientific." "No," the old man answered,
"It knows too much. It says that bitter wars and black
      ruin are necessary: but woe to those
That call them in." "I know," he said, "I have seen
      that.
I was a German." "And now," the old man said, "an
      American?" "No," he answered, "I serve no more.

I serve no more. I tell you: I was designing new weapons
      to save my people: it was not always shameful
To be a patriot: then all went into ruin and the Russians
      coming, we made a choice,
We will go with the West. I hired myself to the American
      Army, my people's enemy,
A mercenary soldier, a man of science, and they gave me
      to work: and I knew well what war
I was preparing."
                He paused and wiped the sweat from
      his pink forehead and said, "But I found some-
      thing.
It was to make a weapon, it is much more. It is a mathe-
      matische Formel, and I tell you
It solves, it solves. It brings under one rule atoms and
      galaxies, gravitation and time,
Photons and light-waves." He fished his pocket and pro-
      duced a black note-book: "I let you see.
You will not understand." The page was lined with sym-
      bols like small dead spiders; one brief equation
Stood pencil-circled. The stubby forefinger struck it and
      the man said, "Your axe it sings: but I tell you
This louder sings." The old man squinted down at it:
      "Not to me. And it is likely
The lost war and much learning have turned you mad.
      But, if the thing were proved, what will you do
With your equation?" "It is," he said, "proved.
Through work of some other men and three cheap experi-
      ments of my own. So I will die and not publish.
I tell you why—this little *Gleichung*, this bite of the mind,
      this little music here,

It can make mortal weapons or immense power, an immense convenience to man: these things I will not.

Science is not to serve but to know. Science is for itself its own value, it is not for man,

His little good and big evil: it is a noble thing, which to use

Is to degrade." "I *see* you are not American," the old man answered, "nor German either." And the other:

"Therefore astronomy is the most noble science: is the most useless." "You are probably mad,"

He answered, "but you think nobly." "So I have cheated," he said, "the American Army and am run away.

Science is not a chambermaid-woman." "Brother," the old man said, "you are right.

Science is an adoration; a kind of worship." "So?" he said,

"Worship?" His round blue eyes behind the bright glasses grew opaque and careful:

"What then is worship?" The old man considered him and said slowly: "A contemplation of God." "*Das noch!*" he answered,

"*Das fehlte noch!* I am a man who thought that even old peasants and leather cowboys after this war

Had learned something." "A coming nearer to God," the old man said slowly. "To learn his ways

And love his beauty." "*Ja,* so," he said, "*der uralte Bloedsinn.* I hope the Russians

Destroy you and your God." Instantly the axe in the old man's hand

Began to scream like a hawk; he huddled it against his thigh, saying "Hush, be quiet. We and the Russians

92

Are," he said, "great destroyers—and God will decide the
        issue. You have perhaps heard some false reports
On the subject of God. He is not dead, and he is not a
        fable. He is not mocked nor forgotten—
Successfully. God is a lion that comes in the night. God
        is a hawk gliding among the stars—
If all the stars and the earth, and the living flesh of the
        night that flows in between them, and whatever is
        beyond them,
Were that one bird. He has a bloody beak and harsh
        talons, he pounces and tears—
And where is the German Reich? There also
Will be prodigious America and world-owning Russia. I
        say that all hopes and empires will die like yours;
Mankind will die; there will be no more fools; wisdom will
        die; the very stars will die;
One fierce life lasts."

                    While he spoke, his axe
Barked like a hunting eagle but incessantly; the old man
        lifted his voice to be heard above it;
The German, stunned by their double clamor, flung up his
        hands to his head and returned away from them
Down the dark silent hill. The gaunt old man on the little
        gray horse
Gazed after him, saying, "God does not care, why should
        I care?" He felt in his mind the vast boiling globes
Of the innumerable stars redden to a deadly starset; their
        ancient power and glory were darkened,
The serpent flesh of the night that flows in between them
        was not more cold. Nothing was perfectly cold,
Nothing was hot; no flow nor motion; lukewarm equality,

93

The final desert. The old man shuddered and hid his face
      and said,
"Well, God has died." He shook like an epileptic and saw
      the darkness glow again. Flash after flash,
And terrible midnight beyond midnight, endless succes-
      sion, the shining towers of the universe
Were and were not; they leaped back and forth like goats
Between existence and annihilation. The old man laughed
      and said,
"Skin beyond skin, there is always something beyond: it
      comes in and stirs them. I think that poor fellow
Should have let in the mad old serpent infinity, the double
      zero that confounds reckoning,
In his equation."

               The axe was still fiercely yelling, the
      old man answered:
"What! After endless time?" He stripped his coat off
And huddled the axe-head in it, and rode down hastily
Behind the stranger. He came to him and said, "Brother:
Because you have chosen nobly between free science and
      servile science: come up with me—
If you are hungry or have to hide from pursuers—
I know every crack of the mountain." But the man would
      not.

37

         The old man heard rumors
Of life and death, and heard that the power of Britain
      was falling in pieces
Like a raft on a reef. "I knew that," he answered,
"At the time of the Boer War.

I saw the most greedy empire gorged and disgorging.
It seems to me that all things happen in my mind
Before they happen."
                    And again: "How beautiful," he
        said, "are these risings
And fallings: the waves of the sea, the Athenian empire,
The civilization of Europe, the might of America. A wave
        builds up,
And it runs toward the shore, higher, higher, higher;
        nothing, you'd say, can resist it; it rakes the stars
        out of heaven;
It spouts a foamhead of empire and dirty wars and drives
        on, toppling and crashing, and it sighs its life out
At the foot of the rock. Slow was the rise,
Rapid the fall: God and the tragic poets
They love this pattern; it is like the beauty of a woman
        to them;
They cannot refrain from it. What goes high they bring
        down. And look—the race of man has become more
        numerous
Than the passenger pigeons, that flattened forests
With the weight of their hordes—but something has hap-
        pened to them suddenly . . .

38

        Dark planets around a dead star, the vultures
Circled, and glided down. The old man came; they perched
        on rocks roundabout, jutting their beaks
And bald red necks, huddling their scrawny bodies
In the broad wings. The carcass had little face and was
        eaten hollow, but the hair on its head

And the hair below the belly were a nubile girl's. The old
     man dismounted and stood
Looking down through the stench; the carcass mumbled
     with its black tongue: "Have pity on me.
Pass your axe through my neck." The old man answered,
     "Surely you are dead and decaying for many days.
Surely a stone is a stone and stone-dead is dead.
Why can you talk?" The black mouth worked and bub-
     bled, it said, "Vee Honsh," and cleared itself and
     said,
"I am dead but I cannot sleep: I am Vere Harnish,
Choked by my mother's blood. Blub-black, blood is black
By candleshine. I ran after her man
Because I loved her. When he unvirgined me
I was horrible to myself, but now I am
More horrible." The old man stood looking down through
     the awful invisible cloud
Of the stench, and said nothing; and again the slime
Crackled and labored in the black throat: "Do you under-
     stand me?
I killed, I killed." He answered, "There has been a war:
     the world is full of people who have killed:
And I do think they sleep." It said: "My mother." "Well,"
     he said, "she was nearest.
It is a need, to kill." "The coyotes," she said, "have been,
     and the wild swine have been, and the vultures
     have been,
And nothing sleeps me: but if you would hew the head
That dreamed it from the hands that did it." He groaned,
     and suddenly
Swung up the double axe, but as it flashed down
The carcass screamed: the man's heart failed, the blade

Hacked the gray earth. He stood gasping and looking
    down, the carcass mumbled,
"Oh, do it do it do it." "Not again," he said. It mumbled,
    "Have mercy on me.
I'll give you my mother's golden eyes." He was silent,
    and said, "Was that
Yellow-eyed one your mother?" "Strike off my head, and
    look
Under my left arm-pit and you will find
Her golden eyes." "What do I want of gold?" "To buy a
    boat,"
It answered, "to buy a boat
When *your* need comes. Oh, strike!" "There is not enough
    gold
In all the West." "But for pity," it said. It screamed
    again,
And he chopped the scream short.
                            He pried up the left shoulder
With his axe-head and found two lumps of speckled gold
On the stained soil. He said, "Perhaps the dead (when
    they talk!) are prophetic, *my* need is coming.
I will go buy a boat."

39

                    He was on the fish-wharf
Buying a boat: a man with white lips and the long eyes
    of terror tiptoed behind him whispering,
"Are you going to escape?" The old man turned and
    made him a sign for silence and whispered,
"I *have* escaped." "Oh," he said, "take me with you, take
    me with you." "But," the old man said, "it is likely

97

I have escaped the things you want, and am seeking
The things you fear. What do you fear?" "The war, the
        war," he said, "the death-rays, the fire-hail,
The horrible bombs." "Certainly," the old man said,
        "there will be a war—
After while. There will be a new ice-age—
After while." "Oh, God," he answered, "more terror!"
            It chanced that a load of ice for the fish-stalls
Had lately passed, and some lumps fallen lay melting: the
        man saw them and shouted, "Oh, God, more terror.
An ice-age comes!" He ran and leaped from the wharf
        and cast himself
Into the sea's cold throat. The old man leaped after him,
And wrestled with him in the choking water,
And saved his life.
            "Why have I done so insanely?" the
        old man said. "It would be better
That twenty million should die than one be saved. One
        man in ten miles is more
Than the earth wants: and clearly this man's life's worth-
        less, being full of fears. I have acted against reason
And against instinct." He laughed and said: "But that's
        the condition of being human: to betray reason
And deny instinct. Did I tell this poor fellow
I had escaped?"
            The man clung to him, as a pilot-fish
Clings to a shark. The old shark groaned and said, "The
        crime and the punishment: because I saved you
I must endure you." But when the boat was boughten and
        they sailed it south, and were off Point Sur,
The man screamed, "I fear shipwreck!" and flung himself

Over the side into the sea's cold throat. The old man
   watched him, and said, "Who am I, that I should
   come
Between man and man's need?" But in a moment he kicked
   the tiller and swung back: "By God," he said,
"I have been in error again; I am full of errors. It is not
   death they desire, but the dear pleasure
Of being saved." He caught the drowner by the hair and
   dragged him
Inboard; who, after he had breathed and vomited,
"Beware," he gasped, "beware, old man, the dear pleasure
Of being Savior." "I am well warned," he answered.

40

So he brought him home; but when they came up the
hill to the house, it was full of people. The old man said,
"Who are you, and where is my dog?" They answered,
"We are refugees. The omens are coughing and sputter-
ing again—
   Woe is the world and all tall cities fall—
so we have fled from the cities, and we found this house
vacant." He said, "Where is my dog?" "There was a
black hound here," they answered, "she bit a child and
ran away."

Then the old man said to his companion, the man of
many terrors: "I have made a bad bargain: I have got a
man and lost a dog. Also I have got a boat and lost a
house: but that bargain's debatable. I shall debate it."

He said to the people in the house: "You are too many
for me to drive you out, even with an axe; and as for me,
I can sleep on the hill. But my friend here is sick, he is

99

sick with many terrors. He is a refugee like you, and you must take him into the house with you." So they did.

Then the old man went and sat on the hill, watching the house, and presently his dog Snapper crept from a bush and joined him. He greeted her, and he said:

"Let us sit here, Snapper, and watch the house. I have put an infection-carrier into it.

I have added fear to the fearful. When they smell his body, even unconsciously, their own fears will stand up and scream.

Terror is more contagious than typhoid, and fear than diphtheria."

So they sat and watched the house; and after three hours the doors burst open; the people fled and were scattered on the mountain, screaming like birds.

The old man said: "Did I call that fellow's life valueless? Nothing is valueless."

41

However, after he had considered the matter more fully, he said: "Nothing is valueless: but some things are obnoxious."

Then truly began the strain of thought. The old man paced back and forth on the hill, sweating and groaning, and at length he said humbly:

"To me."

But even so the matter was not concluded, for the old man's axe in his hand began to spit like a cat, and he stared at it and said proudly: "I agree with you. To *me*. Who has a better right to judge?

God does not judge: God *is*. Mine is the judgment."

42

It was rumored the old man had found gold,
Besides the bits that he had spent for the boat: therefore
       three robbers came up at moondown,
Deep in the night; but the dog Snapper smelled them, the
       axe killed two of them, the old man wakened from
       sleep
And saved the third. He heard the man's teeth clacking,
       and the white dawn stole down the mountain,
He knew him and said, "My man of terrors—is it you?
       Why do you haunt me?" He chattered his teeth
       and said:
"I am your other self. The other half of yourself, white
       of your black. I am always with you."
"Therefore," the old man said, "you betrayed me
To these two thieves. Come," he said, "we must take them
       down to the water. Their bloody corpses here
Would make us trouble."
                   They tied them onto horses
       and led them down; and the old man said,
"Now we must load the boat: here is that need
The damsel spoke of: and let these thieves not lack provi-
       sion
Where they are going." So they laid stones in the boat
       for ballast, and wood for burning, and stretched
       the bodies
On the dry wood: then the old man looked at his com-
       panion, the man of terrors,
Whose hands had never ceased to tremble nor his teeth
       to chatter: "Thrice I have saved his life; now it
       seems

That he is I.—Lean forward," he said to him, "settle the
    log more decently
Under that dead thief's head." Then the man of terrors
Understood fate; and his teeth ceased from rattling, his
    face composed itself: "Sharp," he said, "is your
    mercy,"
And leaned forward over the loaded boat. The old man
    struck once, and fell
On the sand at the boat's tail and lay there senseless
Until the day's end.

                His axe shook off the blood from its
    eyes and stood guard for him, and his dog Snapper
Licked his dead-seeming face. About sundown the old man
    groaned and came to himself, and said,
"It was not easy. Fortunate, Snapper, are all the beasts
    of the mountain: they live their natures: but man
Is outrageous. No man has ever known himself nor sur-
    passed himself until he has killed
Half of himself." He leaned on the boat stern-strake and
    turned his dead man face upward, and the dead
    face
Was his own in his youth. He pulled him higher onto the
    firewood logs, and laid him straight
Between the others; then hoisted sail and struck fire, and
    pushed the boat-stern
Into the purple-shining sea from the sand, and the wind
    was east. The old man, the axe and the dog
Watched from the shore; the boat went softly out to sea,
    flaming
Into the crimson-flaming heart of the sunfall, and its long
    smoke

Mixed with the cloud. The old man laughed with gray
        lips. "There," he said, "goes myself, my self-
        murdered half-self
Between two thieves. It might be some tragic hero's
        death-voyage: Agamemnon's war's end, or world-
        hounded
Hitler's from the lost land he loved and misled
To stinking ruin: that mortal sea-star flaming away to
        the flaming cloud: it is no hero,
But how beautiful it is. Thank you, Vere Harnish."

43

                Rayed and tiger-straked, fire-hearted
Sundown went down; the world was misted, the afterglow
        made its vast rose; one tender color,
Solemn and high and luminous, terribly mournful.
        The old man stared and muttered, "Is it possible
        America's
Bottomless luck has run out at last? We were foolish with
        happiness. We were a generous people
While we enjoyed it."

44

                A scattering pox of insurrections and civil war
Plagued the whole planet; even the patient Russians, a
        palace revolution
Was in the rumors again; even in North America
The pepper and salt of civilization, machine-guns and
        tear-gas, pickled the normal

Discontents of mankind and mistakes of government: and
     what they were doing in holy Asia
Made deserts there.
               The old man was in a Monterey shop,
Fetching his monthly ration, meal, meat and beans, no
     Pythagorean. He heard a yell in the streets,
And looked, and a headless riot was looting the stores.
     He observed them and said,
"Well, I was wrong. America has strained her luck; it
     has not run out yet. It is not the food-stores,
It is the liquor shops and the haberdasher's: happy Amer-
     ica: the luxuries and the vanities,
Whiskey and silk."
               But certain people came to him and
     said: "What shall we do?
For civic order is dying, all men are law-breakers. They
     say you watch the world from your mountain—
     no doubt too high
To see it clearly—" So they mocked him, and said,
"What's your advice?" "Mine?" he said. "It is not new:
     all the rulers know it.
If there's a flea in the water, swallow a toad. If you have
     trouble at home,
Try foreign war." "You are very foolish," they answered,
     "or very wicked." "Both," he said. "But look
How wealthy and how victorious you are. You will not
     labor to avert fate. Fate is your need."

45

When he went home to his mountain the summer cloud
Hid the high places. The old man rode in its fog and said:

104

"I am very foolish or very wicked. It is not little foxes
    crying in the gloom,
It is the children." He turned in the saddle and heard his
    own voice like a blind vulture
Beat through the canyon, bumping against the faces of
    rocks
In the smother of the air, while he said: "Come, little ones.
You are worth no more than the foxes and yellow wolf-
    kins, yet I will give you wisdom.
                              O future children:
Trouble is coming; the world as of the present time
Sails on its rocks; but you will be born and live
Afterwards. Also a day will come when the earth
Will scratch herself and smile and rub off humanity:
But you will be born before that.
                              O future children:
When you are born do not cry; it is not for long.
And when your death-day comes do not weep; you are
    not going far.
You are going to your better nature, the noble elements,
    earth, air and water. That's the lost paradise
The poets remember: I wonder why we ever leave it— Hm?
    What?—Experience.
What an experience."
                    He was silent, and heard the chil-
    dren crying, and he said: "Why?
It is not bad.
There is one God, and the earth is his prophet.
The beauty of things is the face of God: worship it;
Give your hearts to it; labor to be like it.
O future children:

105

Be reticent. Make no display. Let peafowl scream,
And red roses cry, Look at me: they are beautiful: but
        human minds
And bodies are not so pleasing. Therefore be reticent.
Make no display.
                        O future children:
Cruelty is dirt and ignorance, a muddy peasant
Beating his horse. Ambition and power-lust
Are for adolescents and defective persons. Moderate kind-
        ness
Is oil on a crying wheel: use it. Mutual help
Is necessary: use it when it is necessary.
And as to love: make love when need drives.
And as to love: love God. He is rock, earth and water, and
        the beasts and stars; and the night that contains
        them.
And as to love: whoever loves or hates man is fooled in a
        mirror." He grinned and said:
"From experience I speak. But truly, if you love man,
        swallow him in wine: love man in God.
Man and nothing but man is a sorry mouthful."
                                At this time a wind came
And split the cloud. The old man stared up and down
        the enormous unpeopled nave of the gorge and
        laughed again:
"How strange that I cannot see them: but my voice carries
A long way off."

46

                The sun blazed from the west; the old
        man saw his own shadow on his horse's shadow

Wending beside him along the cloud-wall. "Well, it is very
    curious," he said,
"That Worse always rides Better. I have seen in my life-
    time many horsemen and some equestrian statues.
I have observed the people and their rulers; and a circus
    monkey on a Great Dane; and man on the earth."

47

A youth came, and desired to be the old man's disciple.
"But first tell me your name, so that my friends may know
it and listen, when I speak wisely." "My name," the old
man answered, "is Jones or McPherson or some other
word: and what does it matter? It is not true that the
word was in the beginning. Only in the long afternoon
comes a little babble, and silence forever.

"And those," he said, "to whom the word is God: their
God is a word." "Yet I will be your disciple," he answered.

"My conditions," the old man said, "are not easy. My
disciples must never sleep, except the nights when a full
moon sets at midnight."

The young man said, "When is that?" And he con-
sidered and said: "You do not *want* disciples!"

"But how," the old man answered, "did you ever
guess it?"

48

The old axeman slept
In the house dooryard; a saddle—though he rode no more
    —served him for head-rest; he awoke, and the
    night

From the peaks to the sea was a standing pool of prodi-
        gious moonlight: he saw a white-legged woman
Lean over him, gazing at him; her jaw was crooked,
And her mouth splotched with blood; and the white air
Smelled of geraniums. The old man stared upward at her,
And thought—having long ago inquired the story of the
        house—that she was Reine Gore, revisiting
Her scene and sorrow. He reached therefore his arm's
        length her narrow ankle, and felt his fingers
Through the skin and the bone close on mere nothing: as
        one feels the wind
And cannot see it: but here the sense of touch out of use,
The eyes went up the clear white legs to the female hair,
        and up the white belly and the sharp breasts
To the dark dislocation and blood-splatch that were the
        face—but that wried mouth
Labored to speak, not a murmur was heard—therefore
        two senses
Were out of use. And two others active—the intense odor
        of geraniums!—The old man moistened his lips
        and said:
"You are not Reine Gore: that woman is gathered into
        the elements: you are a shell or a token.
Why are you sent?" She waved her long white hands
        toward the northeast, and passed him and glided
        away,
But he observed that she had a shadow.

                                        He thought,
        "What a futile visitor! Why did my mind make
        that?
Or be sensitive to that?—Trouble is coming."

108

49

The horses were lame with age; as for the colts,
The old man was too old to catch them; therefore he went
      on foot
When he went up the mountain. He came to a place of
      dry rocks and wild sun, he saw three vultures
Perched on a crag; they looked as tall as old women, and
      their necks were yellow, their wings like the sails
      of ships
When they unfurled them; they were not common vul-
      tures but condors. The old man stared and said:
      "If *you* are coming back here,
Perhaps the race of man is withering away.
It is a thought; but unlikely."

50

                      "The unique ugliness of
      man and his works," the old man said,
"Seen astronomically, little and whole, in relation with
      time and vastness, the star-world,
And the bitter end waiting for modern man,
Disappears; it falls into pattern with the perpetual
Beauty of things. This is obvious, and this I have learned.
      But the evil, the cruelties, the unbalanced
Excess of pain—that brutal survival-instinct
Tying the tooth to its ache and the man to his cancer—
These damn the race. I do not like the pyres of the
      martyrs.
I do not like barbed wire, squalor and terror. I do not like
      slave-sweat, I do not like torture.

Man invented these things.

It is ignoble," he said, "and
nearly senseless, to pray for anything.

But in so great and righteous a cause—hear me, Lord
God! Exterminate

The race of man. For man only in the world, except a
few kinds of insect, is essentially cruel.

Therefore slay also these if you will: the driver ant,
And the slave-maker ant, and the slick wasp
That paralyzes living meat for her brood: but first
The human race. Cut it off, sear the stump."

So he prayed,
being old and childish, and the Lord answered him
Out of the driving storm: "I will; but not now."

The old man looked at his axe,
For it was neighing like a stallion. "You wish to kill," he
said,

"Every man that we meet. You two-faced violence," he
said, "on the foresweep enemies,

And on the backsweep friends. But that is for God to do,
not for you and me; and he has promised it.
Meanwhile—

To cool your ardor: for I am sick and weary of the
violences

That are done in the world—" He carried the double axe
down to the sea, and whirled it and flung it

From the high cliff; it flew a long flashing arc, dived
gannetlike

And breached the wave: the old man rejoiced and said,
"How quiet we shall be."

But presently the sea boiled,

110

The water blackened and a broad corpse came up, it was
        one of those eight-armed monsters, beaked and
        carnivorous,
That crouch in the cold darkness in the deep sea-caves;
        its bulk was all hacked and mangled, and a fury
        of sharks
Fed on its wounds. But the axe floated clear among the
        shark-snouts,
And swam like a small gray dog in the whirling surf
        under the gull-sky, and came to the cliff and
        climbed it, and came
To the old man's hand.
                     Who gripped the hickory throat
        of the helve and answered: "Is it not enough
What they are doing in Europe and pitiless Asia, but you
        have to chivy
The deep sea also?"

51

        After this his dog left him,
To den with her mate the wolf. He rejoiced and said, "At
        last
The delight of old age: I am alone. Neither dog nor
        woman,
Nor church nor state." But something jerked in his hand,
        he looked down at his axe: "You old gray gnawer,
Be quiet now. Bird with two beaks, two-petalled flower of
        steel, you rank blue flesh-fly
With the two biting wings: will you stop buzzing?
Though you are hungry to hack down heaven and earth,
        it is peace now. We are as old and alone

As the last mammoth in white Siberia,

Mateless, alone, plodding the tundra snow. Here is our
  peace."
    But the axe giggled in his hand,

And presently the great disasters began to fall. The sky
  flashed like a fish's belly, earth shuddered,

And black rain fell. "Perhaps I was wrong," the old man
  said, "I am not alone yet—

But soon to be." The sun's face came red through smoke,

A young man came up the hill in the dark-red light, and
  his livid face

Looked green against it. The old man met him and said,
  "What are you, a mammoth-hunter?" "Are you
  laughing?" he said,

"No one else laughs." "No," he said, "it was my axe. She

Has the last laugh." "Death is hunting us," he answered,
  and suddenly screamed:

"The fire, the blast and the rays. The whiffs of poisoned
  smoke that were cities. Are you utterly merciless?"
  "No,"

He answered, "carefree. I did warn you." "I know you,"
  he screamed,

"You have betrayed us, you have betrayed humanity. You
  are one of those that killed hope and faith,

And sneered at Progress; you have killed the lies that men
  live by, and the earth

Is one huge tomb." "A beautiful one," he answered.
  "Look. Only look. Even in this bad light

What a beautiful one." Then the youth flashed a knife
  and stabbed at him,

But failed through weakness. The old man laughed and
  said, "How they love to be comforted.

Yet," he said, "it is more than comfort: it is deep peace
        and final joy
To know that the great world lives, whether man dies or
        not. The beauty of things is not harnessed to
        human
Eyes and the little active minds: it is absolute.
It is not for human titillation, though it serves that. It is
        the life of things,
And the nature of God. But those unhappy creatures will
        have to shrug off
Their human God and their human godlessness
To endure this time."

52

                    The day like a burning brazen
        wheel heavily revolved, and in the evening
A tribe of panting fugitives ran through the place: the
        old man caught one of them,
Who was too sick to flee. He crouched and vomited some
        green bile and gasped, "God curse the Army,
That got us in, and the air-force that can't protect us.
        They've done it now." "Done," he said, "what?"
        "Rammed their bull-heads
Into the fire-death. This is the end of the world." "Yea?"
        he said. "Of yours, perhaps.
The mountains appear to be on their feet still. And down
        there the dark ocean nosing his bays and tide-
        breaks
Like a bear in a pit. As for the human race, we could do
        without it; but it won't die.

Oh: slightly scorched. It will slough its skin and crawl
 forth
Like a serpent in spring." He moaned and cried out and
 answered, "What is that to me?
I am dying." "Come to the house," he answered, "poor
 man, and rest. You will not certainly die." But the
 man
Coughed blood and died.
　　　　　　　　　　The old man sat down beside
 his body in the blood-brown day's-end
On the dark mountain, and more deeply gave himself
To contemplation of men's fouled lives and miserable
 deaths. "There is," he said, "no remedy.—There
 are *two* remedies.
This man has got his remedy, and I have one. There is no
 third."
About midnight he slept, and arose refreshed
In the red dawn.

SHORTER POEMS

CASSANDRA

T HE mad girl with the staring eyes and long white
        fingers
Hooked in the stones of the wall,
The storm-wrack hair and the screeching mouth: does it
        matter, Cassandra,
Whether the people believe
Your bitter fountain? Truly men hate the truth; they'd
        liefer
Meet a tiger on the road.
Therefore the poets honey their truth with lying; but
        religion-
Venders and political men
Pour from the barrel, new lies on the old, and are praised
        for kindly
Wisdom. Poor bitch, be wise.
No: you'll still mumble in a corner a crust of truth, to men
And gods disgusting.—You and I, Cassandra.

GUARD yourself from the terrible empty light of
      space, the bottomless
Pool of the stars. (Expose yourself to it: you might learn
    something.)

Guard yourself from perceiving the inherent nastiness of
    man and woman.
(Expose your mind to it: you might learn something.)

Faith, as they now confess, is preposterous, an act of will.
    Choose the Christian sheep-cote
Or the Communist rat-fight: faith will cover your head
    from the man-devouring stars.

THAT our senses lie and our minds trick us is true,
        but in general
They are honest rustics; trust them a little;
The senses more than the mind, and your own mind more
        than another man's.
As to the mind's pilot, intuition—
Catch him clean and stark naked, he is first of truth-
        tellers; dream-clothed, or dirty
With fears and wishes, he is prince of liars.
The first fear is of death: trust no immortalist. The first
        desire
Is to be loved: trust no mother's son.
Finally I say let demagogues and world-redeemers babble
        their emptiness
To empty ears; twice duped is too much.
Walk on gaunt shores and avoid the people; rock and
        wave are good prophets;
Wise are the wings of the gull, pleasant her song.

YESTERDAY morning enormous the moon hung
        low on the ocean,
Round and yellow-rose in the glow of dawn;
The night-herons flapping home wore dawn on their wings.
        Today
Black is the ocean, black and sulphur the sky,
And white seas leap. I honestly do not know which day is
        more beautiful.
I know that tomorrow or next year or in twenty years
I shall not see these things—and it does not matter, it
        does not hurt;
They will be here. And when the whole human race
Has been like me rubbed out, they will still be here: storms,
        moon and ocean,
Dawn and the birds. And I say this: their beauty has more
        meaning
Than the whole human race and the race of birds.

PEARL HARBOR

I

HERE are the fireworks. The men who conspired
        and labored
To embroil this republic in the wreck of Europe have got
        their bargain—
And a bushel more. As for me, what can I do but fly the
        national flag from the top of the tower?
America has neither race nor religion nor its own lan-
        guage: nation or nothing.
                                Stare, little tower,
Confidently across the Pacific, the flag on your head. I
        built you at the other war's end,
And the sick peace; I based you on living rock, granite
        on granite; I said, "Look, you gray stones:
Civilization is sick: stand awhile and be quiet and drink
        the sea-wind, you will survive
Civilization."
                    But now I am old, and O stones be modest.
        Look, little tower:
This dust blowing is only the British Empire; these torn
        leaves flying
Are only Europe; the wind is the plane-propellers; the
        smoke is Tokyo. The child with the butchered
        throat
Was too young to be named. Look no farther ahead.

The war that we have carefully for years provoked
Catches us unprepared, amazed and indignant. Our war-
      ships are shot
Like sitting ducks and our planes like nest-birds, both our
      coasts ridiculously panicked,
And our leaders make orations. This is the people
That hopes to impose on the whole planetary world
An American peace.

               (Oh, we'll not lose our war: my
      money on amazed Gulliver
And his horse-pistols.)

               Meanwhile our prudent officers
Have cleared the coast-long ocean of ships and fishing-
      craft, the sky of planes, the windows of light:
      these clearings
Make a great beauty. Watch the wide sea; there is noth-
      ing human; its gulls have it. Watch the wide sky
All day clean of machines; only at dawn and dusk one
      military hawk passes
High on patrol. Walk at night in the black-out,
The firefly lights that used to line the long shore
Are all struck dumb; shut are the shops, mouse-dark the
      houses. Here the prehuman dignity of night
Stands, as it was before and will be again. O beautiful
Darkness and silence, the two eyes that see God; great
      staring eyes.

INK-SACK

THE squid, frightened or angry, shoots darkness
　　Out of her ink-sack; the fighting destroyer throws
　　out a smoke-screen;
And fighting governments produce lies.
But squid and warship do it to confuse the enemy, govern-
　　ments
Mostly to stupefy their own people.
It might be better to let the roof burn and the walls crash
Than save a nation with floods of excrement.

FOURTH ACT

(written in January, 1942)

BECAUSE you are simple people, kindly and ro-
mantic, and set your trust in a leader and
believed lies;
Because you are humble, and over-valued the rat-run his-
torical tombs of Europe: you have been betrayed

A second time into folly. Now fight, be valiant; be cruel,
bloody and merciless, quit you like men.
To fight in a needless war is evil, evil the valor, evil the
victory—to be beaten would be worse.

But fear not that. The little land-frontiered nations are
out of date, the island-empires dissolve;
Only solid continents now can support the oceans of
bombers, the enormous globe of the sky.

It is scene two, act four, of the tragic farce *The Political
Animal.* Its hero reaches his apogee
And ravages the whole planet; not even the insects, only
perhaps bacteria, were ever so powerful.

Not a good play, but you can see the author's intention:
to disgust and shock. The tragic theme
Is patriotism; the clowning is massacre. He wishes to turn
humanity outward from its obsession

In humanity, *a riveder le stelle.* He will have to pile on
horrors; he will not convince you
In a thousand years: but the whole affair is only a hare-
brained episode in the life of the planet.

CALM AND FULL THE OCEAN

CALM and full the ocean under the cool dark sky;
  quiet rocks and the birds fishing; the night-
  herons
Have flown home to their wood . . . while east and west
  in Europe and Asia and the islands unimaginable
  agonies

Consume mankind. Not a few thousand but uncounted
  millions, not a day but years, pain, horror, sick
  hatred;
Famine that dries the children to little bones and huge
  eyes; high explosive that fountains dirt, flesh and
  bone-splinters.

Sane and intact the seasons pursue their course, autumn
  slopes to December, the rains will fall
And the grass flourish, with flowers in it: as if man's world
  were perfectly separate from nature's, private and
  mad.

But that's not true; even the P-38s and the Flying
  Fortresses are as natural as horse-flies;
It is only that man, his griefs and rages, are not what they
  seem to man, not great and shattering, but really

Too small to produce any disturbance. This is good.
  This is the sanity, the mercy. It is true that the
  murdered
Cities leave marks in the earth for a certain time, like
  fossil rain-prints in shale, equally beautiful.

THE Atlantic is a stormy moat; and the Mediter-
        ranean,
The blue pool in the old garden,
More than five thousand years has drunk sacrifice
Of ships and blood, and shines in the sun; but here the
        Pacific—
Our ships, planes, wars are perfectly irrelevant.
Neither our present blood-feud with the brave dwarfs
Nor any future world-quarrel of westering
And eastering man, the bloody migrations, greed of
        power, clash of faiths—
Is a speck of dust on the great scale-pan.
Here from this mountain shore, headland beyond stormy
        headland plunging like dolphins through the blue
        sea-smoke
Into pale sea—look west at the hill of water: it is half the
        planet: this dome, this half-globe, this bulging
Eyeball of water, arched over to Asia,
Australia and white Antarctica: those are the eyelids that
        never close; this is the staring unsleeping
Eye of the earth; and what it watches is not our wars.

EAGLE VALOR, CHICKEN MIND

UNHAPPY country, what wings you have! Even
        here,
Nothing important to protect, and ocean-far from the
        nearest enemy, what a cloud
Of bombers amazes the coast mountain, what a hornet-
        swarm of fighters,
And day and night the guns practicing.

Unhappy, eagle wings and beak, chicken brain.
Weep (it is frequent in human affairs), weep for the ter-
        rible magnificence of the means,
The ridiculous incompetence of the reasons, the bloody
        and shabby
Pathos of the result.

THE persons wane and fade, they fade out of mean-
ing. Personal greatness
Was never more than a trick of the light, a halo of illu-
sion—but who are these little smiling attendants
On a world's agony, meeting in Teheran to plot against
whom what future? The future is clear enough,
In the firelight of burning cities and pain-light of that
long battle-line,
That monstrous ulcer reaching from the Arctic Ocean to
the Black Sea, slowly rodent westward: there will
be Russia
And America; two powers alone in the world; two bulls
in one pasture. And what is unlucky Germany
Between those foreheads?
                                        Observe also
How rapidly civilization coarsens and decays; its better
qualities, foresight, humaneness, disinterested
Respect for truth, die first; its worst will be last.—Oh,
well: the future! When man stinks, turn to God.

HISTORICAL CHOICE

(*written in 1943*)

STRONG enough to be neutral—as is now proved,
  now American power
From Australia to the Aleutian fog-seas, and Hawaii to
  Africa, rides every wind—we were misguided
By fraud and fear, by our public fools and a loved leader's
  ambition,
To meddle in the fever-dreams of decaying Europe. We
  could have forced peace, even when France fell;
  we chose
To make alliance and feed war.

Actum est. There is no returning now.
Two bloody summers from now (I suppose) we shall have
  to take up the corrupting burden and curse of
  victory.
We shall have to hold half the earth; we shall be sick with
  self-disgust,
And hated by friend and foe, and hold half the earth—
  or let it go, and go down with it. Here is a burden
We are not fit for. We are not like Romans and Britons—
  natural world-rulers,
Bullies by instinct—but we have to bear it. Who has kissed
  Fate on the mouth, and blown out the lamp—must
  lie with her.

INVASION

(*written May 8, 1944*)

EUROPE has run its course, and whether to fall by
its own sickness or ours is not
Extremely important; it was a whittled forepeak and con-
densation of profuse Asia, which presently
Will absorb it again. (And if it had conquered eastward
and owned the Urals, would yet be absorbing it.)
Freedom and the lamp have been handed west. Our busi-
ness was to feed and defend them; it was not our
business
To meddle in the feuds of ghosts and brigands in histori-
cal graveyards. We have blood enough, but not for
this folly;
Let no one believe that children a hundred years from
now in the future of America will not be sick
For what our fools and unconscious criminals are doing
today.

But also it is ghastly beautiful. Look:
The enormous weight is poised, primed, and will slide.
Enormous and doomed weight will reply. It is
possible
That here are the very focus and violent peak of all
human effort. (No doubt, alas, that more wasting
Wars will bleed the long future: the sky more crammed
with death, the victims worse crushed: but perhaps
never
Again the like weights and prepared clash.) Admire it
then; you cannot prevent it; give it for emotion

The aesthetic emotion.

                    I know a narrow beach, a thin tide-line
Of fallen rocks under the foot of the coast-range; the
           mountain is always sliding; the mountain goes up
Steep as the face of a breaking wave, knuckles of rock,
           slide-scars, rock-ribs, brush-fur, blue height,
To the hood of cloud. You stand there at the base, perched
           like a gull on a tilted slab, and feel
The enormous opposed presences; the huge mass of the
           mountain high overhanging and the immense
Mass of the deep and somber Pacific.—That scene, sta-
           tionary,
Is what our invasion will be in action. Then admire the
           vast battle. Observe and marvel. Give it the emotion
That you give to a landscape.

                    And this is bitter counsel,
           but required and convenient; for, beyond the
           horror,
When the imbecility, betrayals and disappointments be-
           come apparent—what will you have, but to have
Admired the beauty? I believe that the beauty and noth-
           ing else is what things are formed for. Certainly
           the world
Was not constructed for happiness nor love nor wisdom.
           No, nor for pain, hatred and folly. All these
Have their seasons; and in the long year they balance
           each other, they cancel out. But the beauty stands.

SO MANY BLOOD-LAKES

(written May 12, 1944)

W E have now won two world-wars, neither of
which concerned us, we were slipped in.
We have levelled the powers

Of Europe, that were the powers of the world, into rubble
and dependence. We have won two wars and a
third is coming.

This one—will not be so easy. We were at ease while the
powers of the world were split into factions: we've
changed that.

We have enjoyed fine dreams; we have dreamed of unify-
ing the world; we are unifying it—against us.

Two wars, and they breed a third. Now guard the beaches,
watch the north, trust not the dawns. Probe every
cloud.

Build power. Fortress America may yet for a long time
stand, between the east and the west, like By-
zantium.

—As for me: laugh at me. I agree with you. It is a foolish
business to see the future and screech at it.

One should watch and not speak. And patriotism has run
the world through so many blood-lakes: and we
always fall in.

THE NEUTRALS

NOW the sordid tragedy crashes to a close,
    Blood, fire and bloody slime, all the dogs in the
        kennel
Killing one dog: it is time to commend the neutrals.
I praise them first because they were honest enough
Not to be scared nor bought, and then I will praise them
That their luck held. I praise free Ireland, horse-breeding,
        swan-haunted,
And high Switzerland, armed home of pure snows, and
        Sweden,
High in the north, in the twice-hostile sea: these three
        hold all
That's left of the honor of Europe.
                                    I would praise also
Argentina, for being too proud to bay with the pack,
But her case is not clear and she faced no danger. I will
        praise Finland—
In one poem with the peace-keepers unhappy Finland—
For having fought two wars, grim, clean and doomed.

I HAVE abhorred the wars and despised the liars,
        laughed at the frightened
And forecast victory; never one moment's doubt.
But now not far, over the backs of some crawling years,
        the next
Great war's column of dust and fire writhes
Up the sides of the sky: it becomes clear that we too may
        suffer
What others have, the brutal horror of defeat—
Or if not in the next, then in the next—therefore watch
        Germany
And read the future. We wish, of course, that our women
Would die like biting rats in the cellars, our men like
        wolves on the mountain:
It will not be so. Our men will curse, cringe, obey;
Our women uncover themselves to the grinning victors for
        bits of chocolate.

DAWN

STEEP and black the mountain to the graying sky;
  no star but the morning star
Swims that gray lake. Down here it is deep night; dark
  gleams the surf on the skerries.
West it is night; the great unfaded tapestries of winter
  heaven, Orion and his dog walk north
In the night on the sea. There is nothing on earth nor
  perhaps in the vast of heaven so pure, so desirable
As this hour and this scene.
             Yet the strain sticks. It is a bitter sickness
That rock and water and sky should be what they are, and
  men—what we are. Oh, we escape it sometimes.
But in the shameless floodlights of war and peace, the
  crimes and the lies, the daily news that no doubt
Nobody ought to listen to—but that also would be a kind
  of betrayal—what an ass life looks.
High on the dawn the enormous angular shadow of a sick
  ass being clubbed to death.

C ATTLE in the slaughter-pens, laboratory dogs
Slowly tortured to death, flogged horses, trapped
fur-bearers,
Agonies in the snow, splintering your needle teeth on chill
steel—look:
Mankind, your Satans, are not very happy either. I wish
you had seen the battle-squalor, the bombings,
The screaming fire-deaths. I wish you could watch the
endless hunger, the cold, the moaning, the hope-
lessness.
I wish you could smell the Russian and German torture-
camps. It is quite natural the two-footed beast
That inflicts terror, the cage, enslavement, torment and
death on all other animals
Should eat the dough that he mixes and drink the death-
cup. It is just and decent. And it will increase, I
think.

MOMENTS OF GLORY

THEY have their moments, and if one loved them
　　　　they ought to die in those moments: but
　　　　who could love them?
Consider Churchill contemplating the ditch where his
　　　　great enemy's
Body was burned in the roaring ruin of Berlin—and turn-
　　　　ing away, grinning, making his cockney
Victory-gesture. Consider Hitler prancing stiff-legged
　　　　over fallen France. Consider Harry Truman,
That innocent man sailing home from Potsdam—rejoic-
　　　　ing, running about the ship, telling all and sundry
That the awful power that feeds the life of the stars has
　　　　been tricked down
Into the common stews and shambles.
　　　　　　　　　　　　　　　Contemptible peo-
　　　　ple? Certainly. But how they enjoy their points
　　　　of glory.

WHAT IS WORTHLESS?

AN open secret, the elementary chemistry of Greek
          fire
Scared the barbarian and saved Byzantium.
Civilization stood, the siege was a thousand years, a dead
          tree.
(It is possible this prodigious plutonium
Is our Greek fire once or twice to save us.) The rest was
          prestige and ransom.
Waves of barbarians raved at the wall;
The people yelled at the races; the scholars talked and
          snuffled in the libraries;
The theologians spat at each other;
The artists jewelled their lean art; civilization stood, a
          dead tree.
Was it worth while? What is "worth"? What is worthless?

GREATER GRANDEUR

HALF a year after war's end, Roosevelt and Hitler
          dead, Stalin tired, Churchill rejected—here
          is the
Triumph of the little men. Democracy—shall we say?—
          has triumphed. They are hastily preparing again
More flaming horrors, but now it is fate, not will; not
          power-lust, caprice, personal vanity—fate
Has them in hand. Watch and be quiet then; there is
          greater grandeur here than there was before,
As God is greater than man: God is doing it. Sadly, im-
          personally, irreversibly,
The tall world turns toward death, like a flower to the sun.
          It is very beautiful. Observe it. Pity and terror
Are not appropriate for events on this scale watched from
          this level; admiration is all.

WHAT OF IT?

L IFE'S norm is lost: no doubt it is put away with
        Plato's
Weights and measures in the deep mind of God,
To find reincarnation, after due time and their own de-
        formities
Have killed the monsters: but for this moment
The monsters possess the world. Look: forty thousand
        men's labor and a navy of ships, to spring a squib
Over Bikini lagoon.

           Nobler than man or beast my sea-mountains
Pillar the cloud-sky; the beautiful waters in the deep
        gorges,
Ventana Creek and the Sur Rivers, Mal Paso Creek,
        Soberanes, Garapatas, Palo Colorado,
Flow, and the sacred hawks and the storms go over them.
        Man's fate is like Eastern fables, startling and
        dull,
The Thousand and One Nights, or the jabber of delirium
        —what of it? What is not well? Man is not well?
        What of it?
He has had too many doctors, leaders and saviors: let him
        alone. It may be that bitter nature will cure him.

DIAGRAM

LOOK, there are two curves in the air: the air
      That man's fate breathes: there is the rise and fall
           of the Christian culture-complex, that broke
           its dawn-cloud
Fifteen centuries ago, and now past noon
Drifts to decline; and there's the yet vaster curve, but
           mostly in the future, of the age that began at
           Kittyhawk
Within one's lifetime.—The first of these curves passing
           its noon and the second orient
All in one's little lifetime make it seem pivotal.
Truly the time is marked by insane splendors and agonies.
      But watch when the two curves cross: you children
Not far away down the hawk's-nightmare future: you will
           see monsters.

NEW YEAR'S DAWN, 1947

TWO morning stars, Venus and Jupiter,
Walk in the pale and liquid light
Above the color of these dawns; and as the tide of light
Rises higher the great planet vanishes
While the nearer still shines. The yellow wave of light
In the east and south reddens, the opaque ocean
Becomes pale purple: O delicate
Earnestness of dawn, the fervor and pallor.
—Stubbornly I think again: The state is a blackmailer,
Honest or not, with whom we make (within reason)
Our accommodations. There is no valid authority
In church nor state, custom, scripture nor creed,
But only in one's own conscience and the beauty of things.
Doggedly I think again: One's conscience is a trick oracle,
Worked by parents and nurse-maids, the pressure of the
        people,
And the delusions of dead prophets: trust it not.
Wash it clean to receive the transhuman beauty: then
        trust it.

S EA-LIONS loafed in the swinging tide in the inlet,
      long fluent creatures
Bigger than horses, and at home in their element
As if the Pacific Ocean had been made for them. Farther
      off shore the island-rocks
Bristled with quiet birds, gulls, cormorants, pelicans, hun-
      dreds and thousands
Standing thick as grass on a cut of turf. Beyond these,
      blue, gray, green, wind-straked, the ocean
Looked vacant; but then I saw a little black sail
That left a foam-line; while I watched there were two of
      them, two black triangles, tacking and veering,
      converging
Toward the rocks and the shore. I knew well enough
What they were: the dorsal fins of two killer-whales: but
      how the sea-lions
Low-floating within the rock-throat knew it, I know not.
      Whether they heard or they smelled them, sud-
      denly
They were in panic; and some swam for the islands, others
Blindly along the granite banks of the inlet; one of them,
      more pitiful, scrabbled the cliff
In hope to climb it: at that moment black death drove in,
Silently like a shadow into the sea-gorge. It had the shape,
      the size, and it seemed the speed
Of one of those flying vipers with which the Germans
      lashed London. The water boiled for a moment
And nothing seen; and at the same moment

The birds went up from the islands, the soaring gulls,
      laborious pelicans, arrowy cormorants, a scream-
      ing
And wheeling sky. Meanwhile, below me, brown blood and
      foam
Striped the water of the inlet.

                     Here was death, and with
      terror, yet it looked clean and bright, it was beau-
      tiful.
Why? Because there was nothing human involved, suffer-
      ing nor causing; no lies, no smirk and no malice;
All strict and decent; the will of man had nothing to do
      here. The earth is a star, its human element
Is what darkens it. War is evil, the peace will be evil,
      cruelty is evil; death is not evil. But the breed of
      man
Has been queer from the start. It looks like a botched
      experiment that has run wild and ought to be
      stopped.

ORIGINAL SIN

THE man-brained and man-handed ground-ape,
         physically
The most repulsive of all hot-blooded animals
Up to that time of the world: they had dug a pitfall
And caught a mammoth, but how could their sticks and
         stones
Reach the life in that hide? They danced around the pit,
         shrieking
With ape excitement, flinging sharp flints in vain, and
         the stench of their bodies
Stained the white air of dawn; but presently one of them
Remembered the yellow dancer, wood-eating fire
That guards the cave-mouth: he ran and fetched him, and
         others
Gathered sticks at the wood's edge; they made a blaze
And pushed it into the pit, and they fed it high, around
         the mired sides
Of their huge prey. They watched the long hairy trunk
Waver over the stifle-trumpeting pain,
And they were happy.
                       Meanwhile the intense color and
         nobility of sunrise,
Rose and gold and amber, flowed up the sky. Wet rocks
         were shining, a little wind
Stirred the leaves of the forest and the marsh flag-flowers;
         the soft valley between the low hills
Became as beautiful as the sky; while in its midst, hour
         after hour, the happy hunters

Roasted their living meat slowly to death.

.   These are the people.
This is the human dawn. As for me, I would rather
Be a worm in a wild apple than a son of man.
But we are what we are, and we might remember
Not to hate any person, for all are vicious;
And not be astonished at any evil, all are deserved;
And not fear death; it is the only way to be cleansed.

COMING around a corner of the dark trail . . .
 what was wrong with the valley?
Azevedo checked his horse and sat staring: it was all
 changed. It was occupied. There were three hills
Where none had been: and firelight flickered red on their
 knees between them: if they were hills:
They were more like Red Indians around a camp-fire,
 grave and dark, mountain-high, hams on heels
Squatting around a little fire of hundred-foot logs. Aze-
 vedo remembers he felt an ice-brook
Glide on his spine; he slipped down from the saddle and
 hid
In the brush by the trail, above the black redwood forest.
 This was the Little Sur South Fork,
Its forest valley; the man had come in at nightfall over
 Bowcher's Gap, and a high moon hunted
Through running clouds. He heard the rumble of a voice,
 heavy not loud, saying, "I gathered some,
You can inspect them." One of the hills moved a huge
 hand
And poured its contents on a table-topped rock that stood
 in the firelight; men and women fell out;
Some crawled and some lay quiet; the hills leaned to eye
 them. One said: "It seems hardly possible
Such fragile creatures could be so noxious." Another
 answered,
"True, but we've seen. But it is only recently they have
 the power." The third answered, "That bomb?"

147

"Oh," he said, "—and the rest." He reached across and
     picked up one of the mites from the rock, and
     held it
Close to his eyes, and very carefully with finger and
     thumbnail peeled it: by chance a young female
With long black hair: it was too helpless even to scream.
     He held it by one white leg and stared at it:
"I can see nothing strange: only so fragile." The third
     hill answered, "We suppose it is something
Inside the head." Then the other split the skull with his
     thumbnail, squinting his eyes and peering, and
     said,
"A drop of marrow. How could that spoil the earth?"
     "Nevertheless," he answered,
"They have that bomb. The blasts and the fires are noth-
     ing: freckles on the earth: the emanations
Might set the whole planet into a tricky fever
And destroy much." "Themselves," he answered. "Let
     them. Why not?" "No," he answered, "life."

                                        Azevedo
Still watched in horror, and all three of the hills
Picked little animals from the rock, peeled them and
     cracked them, or toasted them
On the red coals, or split their bodies from the crotch
     upward
To stare inside. They said, "It remains a mystery. How-
     ever," they said,
"It is not likely they can destroy all life: the planet is
     capacious. Life would surely grow up again
From grubs in the soil, or the newt and toad level, and be
     beautiful again. And again perhaps break its legs

On its own cleverness: who can forecast the future?" The
 speaker yawned, and with his flat hand
Brushed the rock clean; the three slowly stood up,
Taller than Pico Blanco into the sky, their Indian-beaked
 heads in the moon-cloud,
And trampled their watchfire out and went away south-
 ward, stepping across the Ventana mountains.

SUPPRESSED POEMS

EDITORS' NOTE

Ten of the following poems were deleted from the Random House edition, apparently at the urging (insistence?) of the editors. That Jeffers had intended their inclusion we know from the original table of contents to the volume, at present housed with the Tor House Papers at the Humanities Research Center, University of Texas, Austin.

The matter of intense disagreement with regard to the content of *The Double Axe*, between Jeffers on the one hand and Saxe Commins and Bennett Cerf on the other, is dealt with in detail by James M. Shebl in his study of *The Double Axe* controversy—*In This Wild Water: The Suppressed Poems of Robinson Jeffers* (Pasadena, Calif.: Ward Ritchie Press, 1976).

In appending these ten poems to the present volume, we have attempted to incorporate the revisions which Jeffers was in the process of making prior to the decision to delete the poems from the volume. In several cases, the originally submitted typescripts are no longer available. While numerous revisions were made after the Random House objections, it is evident that Jeffers made little attempt to accommodate the political sensitivities of the editors. The Random House objections, after all, were not made with regard to the ten poems alone, but rather to the entire import of the volume.

The eleventh poem, "Tragedy Has Obligations," was not included in Jeffers' original typescript. It is from the Tor House Papers at the University of Texas, and

153

was published separately in 1973 by the Lime Kiln Press, the University of California Santa Cruz, with an Afterword by William Everson.

Working from manuscript dates and from evidence within the texts themselves, we have attempted a chronological arrangement of the eleven poems contained in this appendix.

MICHING MALLECHO

(May, 1941)

WAGGING their hoary heads, glaring through
their bright spectacles,
The old gentlemen shout for war, while youth,
Amazed, unwilling, submissive, watches them. This is not
normal,
But really ominous. It is good comedy,
But for a coming time it means mischief. The boys have
memories.

FANTASY

(written in June, 1941)

FINALLY in white innocence
    The fighter planes like swallows dance,
The bombers above ruined towns
Will drop wreaths of roses down,
Doves will nest in the guns' throats
And the people dance in the streets,
Whistles will bawl and bells will clang,
On that great day the boys will hang
Hitler and Roosevelt in one tree,
Painlessly, in effigy,
To take their rank in history;
Roosevelt, Hitler and Guy Fawkes
Hanged above the garden walks,
While the happy children cheer,
Without hate, without fear,
And new men plot a new war.

WILSON IN HELL

(written in 1942)

ROOSEVELT died and met Wilson; who said, "I
  blundered into it
Through honest error, and conscience cut me so deep that
  I died
In the vain effort to prevent future wars. But you
Blew on the coal-bed, and when it kindled you deliberately
Sabotaged every fire-wall that even the men who denied
My hope had built. You have too much murder on your
  hands. I will not
Speak of the lies and connivings. I cannot understand the
  Mercy
That permits us to meet in the same heaven. —Or is this
  my hell?"

TRAGEDY HAS OBLIGATIONS

(*June, 1943*)

IF you had thrown a little more boldly in the flood of
  fortune
You'd have had England; or in the slackening
Less boldly, you'd not have sunk your right hand in Rus-
  sia: these
Are the two ghosts; they stand by the bed
And make a man tear his flesh. The rest is fatal; each day
A new disaster, and at last *Vae Victis,*
It means *Weh den Gesiegten.* This is the essence of trag-
  edy,
To have meant well and made woe, and watch Fate,
All stone, approach.

      But tragedy has obligations. A choice
Comes to each man when his days darken:
To be tragic or to be pitiful. You must do nothing pitiful.
Suicide, which no doubt you contemplate,
Is not enough, suicide is for bankrupt shopkeepers.
You should be Samson, blind Samson, crushing
All his foes, that's Europe, America, half Asia, in his
  fall.
But you are not able; and the tale is Hebrew.

I have seen a wing-broken hawk, standing in her own dirt,
Helpless, a caged captive, with cold
Indomitable eyes of disdain, meet death. There was noth-
  ing pitiful,
No degradation, but eternal defiance.
Or a sheepfold harrier, a grim, grey wolf, hunted all day,
Wounded, struck down at the turn of twilight,

How grandly he dies. The pack whines in a ring and not
closes,
The head lifts, the great fangs grin, the hunters
Admire their victim. That is how you should end—for
they prophesied
You would die like a dog—like a wolf, war-loser.

AN ORDINARY NEWSCASTER

(January 13, 1944)

I heard a radio-parrot, an ordinary newscaster,
    Say this: "Tonight the German astronomers
Will be looking up at the sky: the moon will eclipse the
    planet Jupiter: if our bombers come over
They'll look again." He said with the pride of patriotism,
    "The German astronomers
Are interested in a red spot on Jupiter, they hope the
    eclipse will help them learn something more
About the red spot. But our brave fliers are interested
    only in the red splashes
Made by their falling bombs."

              This is perhaps the most
    ignoble statement we have heard yet, but unfortu-
    nately
It is in the vein. We are not an ignoble people, but rather
    generous; but having been tricked
A step at a time, cajoled, scared, sneaked into war; a
    decent inexpert people betrayed by men
Whom it thought it could trust: our whole attitude
Smells of that ditch. So will the future peace.
              No multibil-
    lion credits, no good will, no almsgiving;
Not even the courage of our young men, bitterly wasted,
    forever to be honored—will be able to sweeten it.

THE BLOOD-GUILT

(*February, 1944*)

SO long having foreseen these convulsions, forecast
the hemorrhagic
Fevers of civilization past prime striving to die, and
having through verse, image and fable
For more than twenty years tried to condition the mind to
this bloody climate:—do you like it,
Justified prophet?

>   *I would rather have died twenty years
> ago.*

"Sad sons of the stormy fall,"
You said, "no escape, you have to inflict and endure . . .
and the world is like a flight of swans."

>   *I said, "No
> escape."*

You knew also that your own country, though ocean-
guarded, nothing to gain, by its destined fools
Would be lugged in.

>   *I said, "No escape."*

>   If you had not
been beaten beforehand, hopelessly fatalist,
You might have spoken louder and perhaps been heard,
and prevented something.

>   *I? Have you never heard
> That who'd lead must not see?*

>   You saw it; you despaired
of preventing it, you share the blood-guilt.

>   *Yes.*

161

RADAR and rocket-plane, the applications of chem-
        istry, the tricks of physics: new cunning
        rather
Than new science: but they work. The time is in fact
A fever-crisis; the fag-end of nominal peace before these
        wars, and the so-called peace to follow them,
Are, with the wars, one fever; the world one hospital;
The semi-delirious patient his brain breeds dreams like
        flies, but they are giants. And they work. The
        question is
How much of all this amazing lumber the pale convalescent
Staggering back toward life will be able to carry up the
        steep gorges that thrid the cliffs of the future?
I hope, not much. We need a new dark-age, five hundred
        years of winter and the tombs for dwellings—but
        it's remote still.

WHAT ODD EXPEDIENTS

G OD, whether by unconscious instinct, or waking,
    or in a dream, I do not know how conscious
    is God,
Uses strange means for great purposes. His problem with
    the human race is to play its capacities
To their extreme limits, but limit its power. For how dull
    were the little planet, how mean and splendorless,
If all one garden; and man locally omnipotent rested the
    energies that only need, only
Bitter need breeds.
                    The solution of course is war, which
    both goads and frustrates; and to promote war
What odd expedients! The crackpot dreams of Jeanne
    d'Arc and Hitler; the cripple's-power-need of
    Roosevelt; the bombast
Of Mussolini; the tinsel star of Napoleon; the pitiful
    idiot submissiveness
Of peoples to leaders and men to death:—what low means
    toward high aims! —The next chapter of the world
Hangs between the foreheads of two strong bulls ranging
    one field. Hi, Red! Hi, Whitey!

SCIENCE, that gives man hope to live without lies
    Or blast himself off the earth:—curb science
Until morality catches up? —But look: morality
At present running rapidly retrograde,
You'd have to turn science too, back to the witch-doctors
And myth-drunkards. Besides that morality
Is not an end in itself: truth is an end.
To seek the truth is better than good works, better than
    survival,
Holier than innocence and higher than love.

WAR-GUILT TRIALS

(*November, 1945*)

THE mumble-jumble drones on, the hangman waits;
    the shabby surviving
Leaders of Germany are to learn that *Vae Victis*
Means *Weh den Gesiegten.* This kind of thing may con-
    sole the distresses
Of Europeans: but for *us*! —Also we've caught
A poet, a small shrill man like a twilight bat,
Accused of being a traitor to his country. I have a bat in
    my tower
That knows more about treason, and about her country.

L|IFE grows, life is not made; you can make death.
        Neither were the sun nor the stars created,
But grew from what grew before. Without the corruption
        of plants and corpses life could not grow.
Look around you at civilization decaying and sick: look
        at science, corrupted
To be death's bawd; and art—painting and sculpture,
        that had some dignity—
Corrupted into the show-off antics of an imbecile child;
        and statecraft
Into the democratic gestures of a gin-muddled butcher-
        boy: look all around you,
And praise the solitary hawk flights of God, and say,
        what a stinking of famous corpses
To fertilize the fields of the human future . . . if man's
        back holds.

166

EDITORS' NOTE TO THE ORIGINAL PREFACE

This preface has been transcribed from Jeffers' type-script worksheets—these in collection at the Humanities Research Center of the University of Texas, Austin. The worksheets actually indicate two prefaces, one short, one long. The shorter of the two is here presented as the initial paragraph, set off by asterisks.

Jeffers' drafts of the original preface present some real problems. There are two pages of handwritten notes, one unnumbered typed page (the short preface), a second unnumbered typed page, a third unnumbered typed page (earlier version of p. 3 of the long preface), a typed page with a number "4" written over with a "2," and four consecutively numbered pages (the long preface), pages two and three being crossed through with diagonal lines. One might conclude, then, that another version of the preface consisted of pages one and four—hence the page four superscribed with a two. The altered page four, then, could actually represent Jeffers' last revision of the material. At the bottom of the page, in pencil, is an acknowledgment of previous publication, presumably of some of the short poems in the volume. The differences in wording may be significant:

It is understood that this attitude is peculiarly un-acceptable at present, being opposed not only by ego-ism and tradition, but by all the currents of the moment. We are now completely trapped in the nets of envy, intrigue, corruption, compulsion, eventual murder, that are called international politics. We have always been expansive, predatory and missionary; and we love to lie to ourselves. We have entered the period of civil struggles and emerging Caesarism that binds republics with brittle iron; civilization everywhere is in its age of decline and abnormal violence. Men are going to be frightened and herded, increasingly, into lumps and masses. A frightened man cannot think; and the mass mind does not want truth—only "Aryan" or "Marxian" or "democratic" or other-colored "truth"—it wants its own flags, not truth. However, the truth will not die; and persons who have lost everything, in the culmination of these evils, and stand beyond hope and almost beyond fear, may find it again.

But if in some future age the dreams of Utopia should incredibly be fulfilled, and men were actually freed from want and fear, then all the more they would need this sanctuary, against the deadly insignificance of their lives, at leisure fully realized. Man, much more than baboon or wolf, is an animal formed for conflict; his life seems to him meaningless without it. Only a clear shift of meaning and emphasis, from man to not-man, can make him whole.

Yet a further version of the preface apparently existed. We have only a single unnumbered page of that, however. The page begins with "government was promoting it" and proceeds to ". . . our intervention in the war of 1939 has been even terribly worse in effect," the passage being identical with the conclusion of the first paragraph in the long preface. The page then continues with a new paragraph, not included in the other version:

These things, I say, were written in that red-brown fog, and under the vicious smoke-screens of deception that mask war-politics, yet I see them being verified, point for point, now that the air has cleared a little;

168

and I have two thoughts on the subject. First: why were my guesses right when others were wrong? Certainly not by virtue of superior intelligence or information, or any prophetic quality

Here the page breaks off, sans period. The typescript is clean; there are no penciled emendations, as is the case with the other worksheets. At least one more page clearly preceded this one. Did that page contain the paragraph here called the short preface as well as the beginning of the long preface? Did something call Jeffers away from the typewriter—in the middle of a sentence? Whatever the case, it seems likely that the poet broke off in the midst of typing the final version of his intended preface, and that the first page is simply missing. It is pure speculation, but perhaps this break-off signaled the moment when Jeffers decided to forgo any lengthy explanation of the over-all intention of *The Double Axe*, to cut it down to the preface which was actually published. And one would be led to conclude, therefore, that it was Jeffers' own final aesthetic determination, rather than any specific pressure from Random House, that caused the poet to lay aside his original preface and instead to settle on the brief "Preface" on Inhumanism that introduces the 1948 edition.

Such a decision, however (if that's what it was), served ultimately to increase the likelihood of incomplete comprehension of the intent and significance of the volume. In his Foreword to James Shebl's *In This Wild Water: The Suppressed Poems of Robinson Jeffers*, R. J. Brophy offers the following commentary:

It might also be argued that the preface was an integral aesthetic part of the volume. Jeffers' custom in pub-

169

lishing was to offer a statement, usually dramatized in a long narrative poem, and to illustrate this theme in its various facets through the shorter poems. Jeffers' prose meditation in *The Double Axe* would have served this same theme-defining function. As it is, the substitute statement, Jeffers' "Preface" on inhumanism, appears to be an afterthought, an answer to the publisher instead of something that forms the original cast of the volume.[1]

1. Robert J. Brophy, Foreword to *In This Wild Water: The Suppressed Poems of Robinson Jeffers,* by James Shebl (Pasadena, Calif.: Ward Ritchie Press, 1976), p. xv.

ORIGINAL PREFACE TO "THE DOUBLE AXE"

* * *

Since my verses have occasionally been spoken of as immoral, anti-religious, (and lately even, a bitter blow, humanist!)—it occurs to me that section 45 of part II of "The Double Axe" might be read as preface to this volume. It seems to express quite briefly the intentions implicit in these poems and previous ones. I take the trouble of this note, not for the sake of the verses, but because it seems to me that the attitude they suggest—the devaluation of human-centered illusions, the turning outward from man to what is boundlessly greater—is a next step in human development; and an essential condition of freedom, and of spiritual (i.e. moral and vital) sanity; clearly somewhat lacking in the present world.

* * *

The first part of "The Double Axe" was written during the war, and finished a year before the war ended. The earliest of the shorter poems were written before America officially entered the war; but it had long been evident that the war was coming, and that our government was promoting it—not with threats, like the Germans, but with pressure and personal promises—and would take part in it. Yet it was equally evident that America's intervention in the European war of 1914 had been bad for America and really fatal for Europe; as it will be clear a few years from now that our intervention in the war of 1939 has been even terribly worse in effect.

But this book is not mainly concerned with the war, and perhaps it ought to be called "The Inhumanist"

171

rather than "The Double Axe." It presents, more explicitly than previous poems of mine, a new attitude, a new manner of thought and feeling, which came to me at the end of the war of 1914, and has since been tested in the confusions of peace and a second world-war, and the hateful approach of a third; and I believe it has truth and value. It is based on a recognition of the astonishing beauty of things, and on a rational acceptance of the fact that mankind is neither central nor important in the universe; our vices and abilities are insignificant as our happiness. We know this, of course, but it does not appear that any previous one of the ten thousand religions and philosophies has realized it. An infant feels himself to be central and of primary importance; an adult knows better; it seems time that the human race attained to an adult habit of thought in this regard. The attitude is neither misanthropic nor pessimist nor irreligious, though two or three people have said so, and may again; but it involves a certain detachment.

A man whose mental processes continually distort and prevent each other, so that his energy is devoted to introversion and the civil wars of the mind, is an insane man, and we pity him. But the human race is similarly insane. More than half its energy, and at the present civilized level nine-tenths of its energy, is devoted to self-interference, self-frustration, self-incitement, self-tickling, self-worship. The waste is enormous; we are able to commit and endure it because we are so firmly established on the planet; life is actually so easy, that it requires only a slight fraction of our common energies. The rest we discharge onto each other—in conflict and charity, love, jealousy, hatred, competition, government, vanity and

172

cruelty, and that puerile passion the will to power—or
for amusement. Certainly human relationships are neces-
sary and desirable; but not to this extent. This is a kind
of collective onanism, pathetic and ridiculous, or at no-
blest a tragic incest, and so I have represented it.

But we have all this excess energy: what should we do
with it? We could take a walk, for instance, and admire
landscape: that is better than killing one's brother in war
or trying to be superior to one's neighbor in time of
peace. We could dig our gardens; the occupation that
seemed to Voltaire's man, after he had surveyed the world,
least foolish. We could, according to our abilities, give
ourselves to science and art; not to impress somebody, but
for love of the beauty that each discloses. We could even
be quiet occasionally.

> Better than such discourse doth silence long,
> Long barren silence square with my desire.

We must always be prepared to resist intrusion; we might
be quiet in the intervals.

Well: do I really believe that people will be content to
take a walk and admire the beauty of things? Certainly
not. I am speaking of a racial disease; it was in the mon-
key blood we derive from, and no doubt it is incurable;
but whoever will can minimize it in his own life. Thoreau's
life was not a bad one; nor Lao-tsze's. The influential
thoughts and books were produced by men meditating
alone; and they were not produced in order to be influ-
ential, nor "to serve humanity," nor for praise or pay,
but because the mind drove. The great work in science was
done by men working alone:—Copernicus, Leeuwenhoek,
Darwin; Newton and Einstein, in youth, when they did

173

their work. The great theorists of atomic structure worked as individuals; only when their work was to be used for mass murder a tight association became necessary.

To sum up the matter:—"Love one another" is a high commandment, but it polarizes the mind; love on the surface implies hate in the depth (Dante who hated well because he loved), as the history of Christendom bitterly proves. "Love one another" ought to be balanced, at least, by a colder saying—this too a counsel of perfection, i.e. a direction-giver, a guide though it cannot be a rule— "Turn away from each other"—to that great presence of which humanity is only a squirming particle. To persons of Christian faith, if any should read this, I would point out that Jesus himself, intuitive master of psychology, invoked this balance. "Love your neighbor as yourself"— that is, not excessively, if you are adult and normal—but "God with all your heart, mind and soul." Turn outward from each other, so far as need and kindness permit, to the vast life and inexhaustible beauty beyond humanity. This is not a slight matter, but an essential condition of freedom, and of moral and vital sanity.

It is understood that this attitude is particularly unacceptable at present, being opposed not only by tradition, but by all the currents of the time. We are now completely trapped in the nets of envy, intrigue, corruption, compulsion, eventual murder, that are called international politics. We have always been expansive, predatory and missionary; and we love to lie to ourselves. We have entered the period of civil struggles and emerging Caesarism that binds republics with brittle iron; civilization everywhere is in its age of decline and abnormal violence. Men are going to be frightened and herded, increasingly,

174

into lumps and masses. A frightened man cannot think; and the mass mind does not want truth:—only "democratic" or "Aryan" or "Marxian" or other-colored "truth":—it wants its own voices. However, the truth will not die; and persons who have lost everything, in the culmination of these evils, and stand beyond hope and almost beyond fear, may find it again.

But if in some future civilization the dreams of Utopia should incredibly be realized, and men were actually freed from want and fear, then all the more they would need this sanctuary, against the deadly emptiness and insignificance of their lives, at leisure fully appreciated. Man, much more than baboon or wolf, is an animal formed for conflict; his life seems to him meaningless without it. Only a clear shift of meaning and emphasis, from man to what is not man, nor a man-dreamed God, a projection of man, can enable him in the long run to endure peace.

"But I having told you"—to quote from the tag of an old poem—have once again and beyond obligation "paid my birth-dues."

AFTERWORD

I

As the reader concludes his reading of this troublesome volume, he will do well to recall what Jeffers himself said in the Preface:

> Its burden, as of some previous work of mine, is to present a certain philosophical attitude, which might be called Inhumanism, a shifting of emphasis and significance from man to not-man; the rejection of human solipsism and recognition of the transhuman magnificence. It seems time that our race began to think as an adult does, rather than like an egocentric baby or insane person. This manner of thought and feeling is neither misanthropic nor pessimist. . . .[1]

Here is a cud to chew on, for the book was found abhorrent by the critics; indeed, one gathers that even the publisher's response was of the same sort. But for this book Jeffers, one of our genuinely great poets, has explicitly announced a lofty and philosophic intention; and, successful or not, *The Double Axe* is at the very least an astounding document. How then does one match the book itself to its professed intention?

The first narrative details a resurrected destroying prodigal who has returned to murder his father and, almost incidentally and yet inevitably, to possess his mother, discovering in his return that he must slay a former

---

1. Robinson Jeffers, *The Double Axe and Other Poems* (New York: Random House, 1948; Liveright, 1977), p. vii (xxi). All other references to *The Double Axe* will be given by page number only.

friend as well, one who has become his mother's lover. The central piece, "The Inhumanist," depicts adultery, hatred of daughter for mother (owing to sexual jealousy), multiple rape and whipping, attempted suicide and seduction of stepfather by daughter, the old man severing the head of the still-speaking body of that daughter (apparently her second suicide attempt was more successful) following her murder of the mother, the old man's slaying of the ghost of his youth, a plea to God to exterminate the race of man, and a day of worldwide atomic hellfire. And, finally, we have the two concluding short poems, "Original Sin" and "The Inquisitors." The first of these depicts Rousseau's "noble savage" as "The most repulsive of all hot-blooded animals / Up to that time of the world,"[2] a creature which utilizes significant cunning combined with discovery not merely for the purposes of survival but also for the torturing to death of a caught mammoth. The second of these poems portrays three great autochthonous giants, earth spirits, that look at the human beings they have caught and are filled with wonder that "Such fragile creatures could be so noxious," and, splitting open the skull of one, find only "A drop of marrow. How could that spoil the earth?"[3]

And yet the author has told the reader that "This manner of thought and feeling is neither misanthropic nor pessimist. . . ." It would be difficult not to believe, then, that Jeffers' "lover's quarrel" with humanity is here delineated at its most excruciatingly incandescent. The unbridled and savage anger of "The Love and the Hate" is obvious to any reader. The concluding poems, "Origi-

2. "Original Sin," p. 145.
3. "The Inquisitors," pp. 147–148.

178

nal Sin" and "The Inquisitors," present as it were a before-and-after object lesson. The human flaw was inherent; spoliation of the earth awaited only the time requisite for the absurd apes that dropped from trees and ruled for a time to acquire sufficient knowledge to ram "their bull-heads / Into the fire-death."[4]

But even in the "fire-death" at the conclusion of "The Inhumanist," Jeffers does not imagine an end to humanity. The old Inhumanist tells us: "As for the human race, we could do without it; but it won't die. / Oh: slightly scorched. It will slough its skin and crawl forth / Like a serpent in spring."[5] Jeffers' account of the night following the day of destruction is joltingly brief, a night during which the old man gives himself "To contemplation of men's fouled lives and miserable deaths." In conclusion, the old man asserts, "There is . . . no remedy.—There are two remedies."[6] The first of these is death, "the only way to be cleansed," as the poet says in "Original sin." The second is Inhumanist endurance: ". . . and there is endurance, endurance, death's nobler cousin. Endurance."[7] And so humanity, that "botched experiment that has run wild and ought to be stopped,"[8] endures, survives. As for the Inhumanist, "About midnight he slept, and arose refreshed / In the red dawn."[9]

The red dawn: is it the dawn of total and annihilating atomic conflagration or a return and reassertion of natural order, and hence the beginning of a new human age,

4. P. 113.
5. Pp. 113–114.
6. P. 114.
7. P. 81.
8. "Orca," p. 144.
9. P. 114.

with humanity, slightly scorched, having sloughed its skin and crawling forth "like a serpent in spring"? Apparently the latter—but let us turn to a thematic analysis of "The Inhumanist."

II

"The Inhumanist" is, in many ways, central to Jeffers' work, in that it delineates in summary fashion both the nature of the Inhumanist quest and the various residual obstacles confronting one who has pursued the quest throughout youth and middle age and into old age—the latent but nonetheless real "obscure human fidelities"[10] that continue at moments to perplex even one who has effectively passed beyond them. The old man, the Grail-seeker, is both an idealization and a caricature of Jeffers himself—an idea which will amaze no one, I think, who is familiar with the body of this poet's work.

I would find literary precedent in several works by other writers. The old man is rather a Jude the Obscure figure, but one who has learned something and who has lived rather than died—one who has grown old and who has absented himself from the flux and flow of humanity—one indeed who rejects tragedy as a human-centered form and who finally comprehends the inexorable cycles as being beyond tragedy, a condition which Jeffers' earlier figure of Orestes presumably reached. But *The Tower Beyond Tragedy* does not reveal the nature of this condition: it is left to the imagination, one would hazard a guess, simply because the poet himself was not at that

10. "Obscure human fidelity" is the reason Jeffers gives for California's shooting of the horse in *Roan Stallion*. *The Selected Poetry of Robinson Jeffers* (New York: Random House, 1938), p. 157.

180

time in his own life close enough to the realization of it to record it fully.

But the figure of the stonemason Jude merely contained the potential of the old Inhumanist—nothing of its realization. The literary precedents I would suggest are these: Sophocles' *Philoctetes*, Shakespeare's *Timon of Athens*, Byron's "Darkness," Shelley's "The Triumph of Life," and Eliot's *The Waste Land*. In none are the parallels exact, but in all of them one can find something of the same vision and impulse, as well as some of the same stage properties: the weapon in *Philoctetes*, the finding of gold in *Timon* (the old man, of course, is merely rumored to have found it), the faithful dog in "Darkness," the onward course of human futility and self-destruction, with moral victory presumably earned by the few, in "The Triumph of Life," and the Tiresias-like figure of the seer, complete with a presumed solution or way out of the human desert of *The Waste Land*.

In both *Philoctetes* and *Timon of Athens* we find the figure of the isolate, the exile, living in a cave—while the old man has assumed the role of caretaker for the abandoned Gore house. Philoctetes and Timon learn to exist in harmony with an order of nature, even as the old man does. Philoctetes would like to go home; Timon has no such intention. Both would drive intruders away. In the old Inhumanist we find a combination of these characteristics. Philoctetes, at the command of the ghost of Heracles, will rejoin the Greek forces, and Troy will fall, so the legend runs, partially owing to the presence of his invincible weapon. Timon will not return but rather will die in his self-chosen isolation.

But "The Inhumanist" is hardly to be regarded as derivative. Unlike Philoctetes or Timon, the old man (as

181

I have suggested) is a Grail-seeker—more exactly, a
God-seeker. Without question it is the search for God in a
time of coming catastrophe, and in full view of the whole
horror of recorded human existence, the perpetual war-
fare, the dim fumblings toward freedom, the inevitable
opting for security rather than freedom, the corruptions
of power and the disruptive sexual urgings, all the various
manifestations of human cruelty and filth and supersti-
tion—it is this search for God which informs the poem.
What we are given to see are the Inhumanist's final over-
comings, his final breaking free from the last holds which
humanity has upon him.

This ultimate transcendence, appropriately enough, is
framed against human-triggered destruction on an im-
mense scale. Unlike Byron's "Darkness," the end of the
world (the human world in this case) is only sketched in:
it is purposely kept out of the Inhumanist's immediate
purview. Byron's night is to be unending: Jeffers' night
passes quickly, and, along with the Inhumanist, we as
readers are ushered "refreshed" into "the red dawn."

Ultimately, of course, the entirety of the universe will
be destroyed: but a new universe will form. For the im-
mediate present, the circles interpenetrate. The old man
envisions that "Wildcat, coon and coyote, deer and wild
pig, weasel and civet-cat, the stalking puma and the
dainty foxes, / Traveled together, they all went the one
way"[11] around the mountain; in the opposite direction
flow the races of humanity. The beasts move into the past,
humanity into the future. But the old man asserts, "I
would break both my legs / Liefer than go with beasts or

11. P. 84.

men or angels *en masse.*"[12] In any case, both circle the
mountain, and time is a ring. The Inhumanist says to
humanity, ". . . when again you meet the beasts on this
pleasant hill . . . / I shall be here."[13]

In the Foreword to the present volume, Everson has
suggested that in the old Inhumanist, Jeffers has created
"something suspiciously like a savior figure," one who
"constitutes [a] model for human conduct."[14] Yet the old
man rejects the idea of *en masse,* even as he rejects the
paradigm of the savior: "By God . . . / I have been in
error again; I am full of errors. It is not death they
desire, but the dear pleasure / Of being saved."[15] He has
rescued (for a second time) the young man of fears, the
ghost of his own youth. The young man immediately
gasps, ". . . beware . . . the dear pleasure / Of being
Savior," to which the Inhumanist answers, "I am well
warned."[16] Finally the old man will realize his own neces-
sity and will slay this doppelgänger, asserting, "No man
has ever known himself nor surpassed himself until he has
killed / Half of himself."[17] Later a youth comes to be his
disciple, only to be turned away. When the youth dis-
covers that the Inhumanist wants no disciples, the old
man says, "But how . . . did you ever guess it?"[18]

The Inhumanist is the Savior in spite of himself and
was consciously proposed as such by the poet. He is a
Carlylean hero: selected individuals may learn from him
and may follow in his footsteps but only by means of find-

12. P. 85.
13. P. 85.
14. William Everson, Foreword, p. xvii.
15. P. 99.
16. P. 99.
17. P. 102.
18. P. 107.

ing their own paths. Jeffers' argument with the assumptions of humanism and with any set of schemes for the betterment of humanity, whether religious or political, is that such schemes constitute a species of group-think and are therefore inherently unworkable for the individual. Barclay, the hero of Jeffers' *The Women at Point Sur*, allows his quest for truth to be corrupted by his needs for disciples and for sexual gratification—and the result is madness.

The Inhumanist does not allow this to happen, and he remains sane—gains sanity—and emerges whole. In *Point Sur*, Jeffers said that he would sometime ". . . fashion images great enough to face [God] / A moment and speak while they die."[19] The old Inhumanist is such a figure. Even in old age, however, the "obscure human fidelity" continues to draw at him; and so, like Everyman, he stumbles toward the place of salvation, for Jeffers the condition of "organic wholeness," his mind growing ever more clear. Truth and beauty alone are the final values, for these represent the condition of God. Man is a part of this wholeness, despite his sorry record, and hence must be accepted.

The old man speaks to the children of the coming age, advising them in part:

O future children:
Cruelty is dirt and ignorance, a muddy peasant
Beating his horse. Ambition and power-lust
Are for adolescents and defective persons. Moderate
     kindness
Is oil on a crying wheel: use it. Mutual help

19. *The Women at Point Sur* (New York: Boni & Liveright, 1927; Liveright, 1977), p. 73.

Is necessary: use it when necessary.

. . .

> But truly, if you love man,
> swallow him in wine: love man in God.
> Man and nothing but man is a sorry mouthful.[20]

In this sense, as Everson says, "the salvific instance has been achieved."[21] Mankind moves *en masse*, but the individual may find wholeness in the proper contemplation of God, even though death "is the only way to be cleansed."

The conceptual content of "The Inhumanist" might well have been recorded in a sequence of philosophical meditations, after the fashion of Marcus Aurelius, and yet Jeffers chose to utilize the figure of the old man and his cast of supporting characters in what amounts very nearly to the mode of the morality play. The reason for this, no doubt, has to do with Jeffers' being essentially a dramatic poet rather than a systematic philosopher, the assumption being that an idea whose implications are enacted is kept more certainly within the human context and is hence ultimately more meaningful to the reader. With this concept in mind, then, it will behoove us as readers to give careful examination to the dramatic sequences as they are presented.

III

Inhumanism proposes two codes, one dependent upon the other. First, through the contemplation of the transhuman magnificence of natural beauty, one may uncenter one's vision and thereby achieve an essentially nonhuman

20. P. 106.
21. Everson, Foreword, p. xviii.

perspective. Second, since the human condition absolutely implies human contacts and loyalties, human fidelities as well as participation in those drives which are inherent to the race, one must learn the lesson of Stoic endurance, with its resultant possibility of moral victory. Indeed, in order to free the mind for the contemplation of natural beauty and, through it, for the contemplation of the Divinity which has created that beauty, it is imperative that one learn first to endure. But how?

The metaphor that Jeffers uses here is that of the double-bit axe, for with it one may cut away the errors and even the obligations of the past, just as one may cut away the fears of the future and of death. To be truly non-human would be to need no such axe; to be human requires a weapon. And to use such an axe demands great courage—as well as a nonhuman-centered view. The axe, as the old man says, is "A blade for the flesh, a blade for the spirit: and truth from lies."[22]

With this blade the old man will sever the head from the dead body of Vere Harnish, as the dead girl has wished. In this action the Inhumanist learns that apparent cruelty may in fact be kindness—and he learns nonhuman strength. When he finally uses the same blade on the man of fears, falls senseless with his axe standing guard, and then comes once more to his senses and sends the body ". . . out to sea, flaming / Into the crimson-flaming heart of the sunfall," he is able to say, "Thank you, Vere Harnish."[23]

After having pleaded with God to exterminate the race

22. P. 54.
23. Pp. 102–103.

of man, and after having heard the voice of God out of
the driving storm say, "I will; but not now," the old man
hears his axe neighing like a stallion:

"You wish to kill," he said,
"Every man that we meet. You two-faced violence,"
  he said, "on the foresweep enemies,
And on the backsweep friends. But that is for God to
  do, not for you and me; and he has promised
  it."[24]

The Inhumanist flings the axe out into the sea and
imagines peace, but the blade strikes a monster of the
deep, which rises to the surface like Tennyson's Kraken,
to be devoured by sharks. The axe floats to the surface,
swims to shore, and climbs back to the old man's hand.
The inherent violence of the unconscious is devoured by
the violences of the conscious self, but even so, the In-
humanist must address his weapon:

"You old gray gnawer,
Be quiet now. Bird with two beaks, two-petalled
  flower of steel, you rank blue flesh-fly
With two biting wings: will you stop buzzing?
Though you are hungry to hack down heaven and
  earth, it is peace now. We are as old and alone
As the last mammoth in white Siberia. . . .[25]

The axe, however, giggles: and the day of atomic hell-
fire is touched off. The weapon has a will of its own; its
double blade is not specific but rather universally human.
The axe, ultimately, is the two-hemisphered human brain,
and it has created this time of holocaust: "The day like a
burning brazen wheel heavily revolved, and in the eve-

24. P. 110.
25. Pp. 111–112.

ning / A tribe of panting fugitives ran through the place. . . ."[26]

From the very beginning, the Inhumanist is in search of his "red dawn." The poem opens with its first several sections given to a contemplation of the existence and nature of the Divinity, defining a proposed deity which is "Not a tribal nor an anthropoid God," one which is conscious, one which has generated a cosmos in which there is nothing that is not "alive," and one which is immortal, even though the cosmos itself is primarily characterized by unending change: "The hills dissolve and are liquidated; the stars shine themselves dark."[27]

A dog comes to the old man; in kindness, he feeds it— it returns, choosing security rather than freedom. She is to be his companion, along with the axe and along with his illegitimate daughter, Gaviota, Sea-gull. The bitch will finally take a wild lover, for "Dogs and men tire of a slow decline."[28] She will leave the old man, to nest with her coyote, just before the axe giggles its atomic rainstorm.

The daughter, as well, will go with her wild lover, Clive Enfield, having first been raped and whipped because of Mrs. Enfield's desire for revenge upon this girl her husband prefers to her. Indeed, her very presence is disturbing to the old man, for though she is his daughter, his sexual drive is awakened. In the middle of the night Gaviota finds her father grinding an old axe:

> Working the treadle grindstone behind the house,
>   grinding an axe, leaning the steel on the stone

26. P. 113.
27. Pp. 52–54.
28. P. 80.

So that it screamed, and a wild spray of sparks
Jetted on the black air.[29]

The old man is able to transcend his desire, however, and
tells his daughter:

But I will be turned again to the
outer magnificence, the all but inhuman God.
I will grind no more axes.[30]

At the moment of her leaving with Clive, Gaviota crushes
"the fine grapes of her breasts" against her father's ribs,
and he tells Enfield, "Look here, young man: / Give her
a baby soon or she'll melt the rocks. . . ."[31]

An even more powerful expression of the theme of sex-
ually engendered disquietude, however, lies in the person
of the cruelly jealous wife of Clive Enfield, Dana—for
her possessive desire for her husband is neurotically in-
tense. And the issue is further complicated by the fact
that her daughter, Vere Harnish, is apparently in love
with the same man. When the storm-driven pelican, a
powerful mother symbol, crashes through the window,
Vere stabs the bird to death in an action that prefigures
her murder of the mother. Having plunged a penknife
repeatedly into the bird's bloody breast, she says, "It
smells like fishblood, it nearly mothers me."[32] It may well
be that Dana's horrible thirst for revenge upon Gaviota

29. Pp. 81–82.
30. P. 82.
31. P. 86.
32. P. 69. Some have seen "mothers" as a typographical
error, with the correct rendering as "smothers." But Jeffers did
not correct this in his personal copy. In Vere's distempered
mind, in any case, "mother" and "smother" are seen as the same.
The killing of the bird and the subsequent matricide are dealt
with in parallel fashion. Hence, I conclude that "mothers" was
the word Jeffers intended.

189

is partially derived from displaced aggression against her daughter; indeed, it might be argued that Vere and Gaviota are themselves doppelgängers. In any case, this primary example of sexually derivative madness is kept at a distance from the old Inhumanist himself. Even after the rape and whipping, Gaviota does not tell her father what has happened.

The theme of the intolerable strain of the human condition, dealt with at great length in *The Women at Point Sur,* is also an effective portion of "The Inhumanist." The old man feels this tension even as he moves away from its implications. He tells us:

> . . . all the galactic universes
> Are organized on one pattern, the eternal round-
> about, the heavy nucleus and whirling electrons,
> the leashed
> And panting runners going nowhere; frustrated
> flight, unrelieved strain, endless return—all—
> all—
> The eternal fire-wheel.[33]

In contemplation of this, the Inhumanist hears (or imagines he hears) the voice of God crying out, "I am caught. I am in the net. . . . / I see my doom." The old man laughs and imagines that an Oedipus or a Lear has given issue to the ghostly voice, toys with the idea that human passion ". . . is only a reflex of / Much greater torment. . . ."[34] But he hardens his mind to the idea and builds a cairn to "Nicky Kupernick," the first to push man "Out of his insane self-importance and the world's navel, and taught him his place."[35] He then proposes to build another in honor of Darwin.

33. P. 67.
34. Pp. 67–68.
35. P. 72.

He strengthens his resolve for endurance and then, having ground down his old axe of sexual (incestuous) temptation, he further resolves to pass beyond tragedy: "Every tragic poet has believed it possible. And every Savior, Buddha down to Karl Marx, / Has preferred peace. Tragedy, shall we say, is a cult of pain, and salvation of happiness."[36] Given the human perspective, tragedy has a function: it gives us the scapegoats, even as Jeffers had earlier theorized in "Apology for Bad Dreams." But to pass beyond humanity is to pass beyond the need for tragedy, and the Inhumanist says, "I will grind no more axes." This protagonist will not go mad; and the poem itself will draw on to its conclusion, not as a tragedy but, insofar as is consonant with the Jeffers world view and the needs of this extended parable or morality play, as a comedy—a comedy replete with the near annihilation of humanity. Gaviota and her lover go off to discover whatever kind of life their love will engender, and the old Inhumanist will survive even doomsday.

A paragraph from R. J. Brophy's *Myth, Ritual, and Symbol* may at this point be read to good advantage:

> Tragedy is not the end but the means; it is to be left behind as soon as the end is achieved. From inside the tragedy (as actual protagonist), Orestes works free from pity and fear. From the outside (vicarious participation), the artist and the reader do the same. Nothing is further from the intent of Jeffers' art than empathy; purging pity and fear means dismissing them, moving beyond them. If tragedy in Jeffers' sense means moving away from pity and fear, the title

36. P. 83.

"Tower Beyond Tragedy" could be interpreted: "Tower Beyond Time Achieved by Tragedy."[37]

It is precisely beyond pity and fear that the Inhumanist must move—beyond pity and fear and sexual desire. But to move beyond pity is perhaps the hardest requirement of all. The old man envisions the children of the future:

> When you are born do not cry; it is not for long.
> And when your death-day comes do not weep; you
>   are not going far.
> You are going to your better nature, the noble ele-
>   ments, earth, air and water. That's the lost
>   paradise
> The poets remember.
>
> .   .   .
>
> There is one God, and the earth is his prophet.
> The beauty of things is the face of God: worship it;
> Give your hearts to it; labor to be like it.[38]

The ghost of sexual desire appears to him once more, in the guise of Reine Gore, and "He reached therefore his arm's length her narrow ankle, and felt his fingers / Through the skin and bone close on mere nothing. . . ." His eyes ". . . went up the clear white legs to the female hair, and up the white belly and the sharp breasts / To the dark dislocation and blood-splatch that were the face. . . ." He imagines that she is a phantom sent to vex him, and "she waved her long white hands toward the northeast, and passed him and glided away, / But he observed that she had a shadow."[39] He wonders why his

37. Robert J. Brophy, *Robinson Jeffers: Myth, Ritual, and Symbol in His Narrative Poems* (Cleveland and London: Case Western Reserve University Press, 1973), p. 151.

38. P. 105.

39. P. 108.

mind has created the vision—says to himself, "Trouble is coming." Three condors appear, and the Inhumanist wonders if ". . . the race of man is withering away. / It is a thought; but unlikely."[40]

The trouble that comes, if triggered by the giggling axe, is nonetheless precisely a human invention. A young man climbs up the hill, screaming, "The fire, the blast and the rays. The whiffs of poisoned smoke that were cities. Are you utterly merciless?" The Inhumanist asserts simply, "I did warn you." But the young man proceeds to indict the Inhumanist:

You have betrayed us, you have betrayed humanity.
    You are one of those that killed hope and faith,
And sneered at Progress; you have killed the lies that
    men live by, and the earth
Is one huge tomb.[41]

Such is the indictment, and as such it was echoed by the critics. But the complaint is a foolish, even a pathetic one, for men cannot live by lies, and the spelling of "Progress" with an upper-case letter is in effect to deify it and hence to turn it into one of the greatest lies of all. The Inhumanist asserts merely that:

                    . . . it is deep peace and final joy
To know that the great world lives, whether man dies
    or not. The beauty of things is not harnessed to
    human
Eyes and the little active minds: it is absolute.
It is not for human titillation, though it serves that.
    It is the life of things,
And the nature of God. But those unhappy creatures
    will have to shrug it off

40. P. 109.
41. P. 112.

Their human God and their human godlessness
To endure this time.[42]

And it is true, of course. We have been warned. At the present time, it is most assuredly certain that Jeffers is hardly alone in delivering such a message; indeed, dooms- day and post-doomsday literature has developed to such an extent as to have defined itself as a literary genre. But the effect of the warning? Well, we haven't set off the big bombs yet. And perhaps now that we have gotten used to the central ideas, it will be possible for a new generation of readers to transcend its revulsion with regard to the content of *The Double Axe* and hence to see the poems clearly. Even now it will be difficult—a difficulty which Jeffers perceived quite accurately. As the poet says to Cassandra:

> Poor bitch, be wise.
> No: you'll still mumble in a corner a crust of truth, to men
> And gods disgusting.—You and I, Cassandra.[43]

BILL HOTCHKISS

42. P. 113.
43. "Cassandra," p. 117.

TEXTUAL NOTE

In verifying the text of *The Double Axe*, we are deeply indebted to Dr. David Farmer of the Humanities Research Center, University of Texas, Austin, who, with his staff, researched six "suspect" passages against the manuscripts. To quote Dr. Farmer, "Everything seems to be just as given."

On our own authority alone, then, we have changed "tasting out the old thirty-thirty" to "testing out the old thirty-thirty," for this must certainly be a typist's error (p. 13).

In one further place we have also altered the text of the 1948 edition, which read, "the last mammoth in old Siberia." This we have changed to "the last mammoth in white Siberia," our authority being Jeffers himself, for he penned in this correction in his personal copy of the book. Donnan Jeffers has verified the change as being in his father's handwriting. The reason for this post-publication alteration is obvious in context, for the word "old" has been used just eight words previously (p. 112).

Two other suspect passages may be worthy of note. The first of these reads, "He was showing me / His wounds. I mean his wounds" (p. 23). Jeffers sometimes utilizes the Freudian slip device, and that would seem to have been the intention here—but the manuscript verifies the line as is. The second problematical passage reads, "It smells like fishblood, it nearly mothers me" (p. 69). Should this be "smothers" instead of "mothers"? Vere has just stabbed the pelican to death, an action she will later repeat upon the person of her mother; indeed, in slaying the pelican, she symbolically slays the mother. It makes sense, and the manuscript verifies it.

In verifying the texts of the ten poems deleted from the 1948 edition, we are again indebted to David Farmer of the Humanities Research Center, University of Texas, Austin. We are also indebted to James M. Shebl (*In This Wild Water: The Suppressed Poems of Robinson Jeffers*) and to Robert Ian Scott, who has also done a set of transcriptions.

Our readings, which occasionally differ from the versions published in Shebl's book, are based upon Jeffers' numbered typescripts, from the Texas collection. We have departed from these numbered typescripts only to the extent of placing the phrases *Vae Victis* and *Weh den Gesiegten* in italics, these being used in both "War-Guilt Trials" and "Tragedy Has Obligations."

An unnumbered typescript of "The Blood-Guilt" (with emendations) contains a final deleted line which reads: "Buchenwald and Lidice and Bataan will not be remembered—nor Hiroshima forgotten." While Jeffers was obviously still working on the poem in 1945, a handwritten version of the poem is dated February, 1944. An alternate ending reads, "Now that all men shout war, what will you say? ~~Civil war. Nothing.~~ War." This, too, is deleted.

Scott's reading of "What Odd Expedients," apparently taken from an unnumbered typescript with a welter of emendations and a great deal of crossing out, ends with the following: "The next chapter of the world / Concerns America and Russia, two bulls in one pasture.

Structure is broken between their foreheads, new things are born."

Shebl notes that Jeffers' original table of contents used the title "Look All around You" rather than "Pourvou Que Ça Doure," an idiomatic phrase meaning "provided that it lasts." The former title was, according to Shebl, ". . . changed by Jeffers as he less than earnestly attempted to 'revise' some of the poems. All notes indicate he would go with this [the latter] title; it works well thematically and formally."

The text of "Tragedy Has Obligations" was transcribed from Jeffers' worksheets by William Everson.

Finally, one might note Jeffers' use of *Vae Victis* and *Weh den Gesiegten* in both "Tragedy Has Obligations" and in "War-Guilt Trials." The German phrase ("Woe to the conquerors") stands in ironic contrast to the well-known words of Brennus, the king of the Gauls, in dealing with the conquered Romans: "Wehe den Besiegten," essentially a transliteration of "Vae Victis"—"Woe to the vanquished."